LONG SHOTS

Jay Wright, Villanova, and College Basketball's Most Unlikely Champion

Dana O'Neil

TRIUMPH
B O O K S

Library of Congress Publication Data available upon request.

This book is available in quantity at special discounts for your group or organization. For further information, contact:

Triumph Books LLC
814 N. Franklin
Chicago, Illinois 60610
www.triumphbooks.com

Printed in United States of America
ISBN: 978-1-62937-459-8
Design by Patricia Frey
Photos courtesy of AP Images unless otherwise indicated

*To Madigan and Kieran, who make this long-shot
mom look like a champion every day.*

Contents

Foreword

For many years, I had the honor and privilege of sitting courtside to call Big Monday games on ESPN with broadcast legends Bill Raftery and Sean McDonough. The three of us always looked forward to Big Monday, in part because we were together, and in large part because we were going to witness an old-school, bare-knuckle Big East brawl that had championship tradition, blood rivalry, and some of the finest players and coaches in the game's history behind it. We never had to explain the meaning of Big Monday to anyone. We just had to say, "Big Monday."

When we first started working together, Raftery, McDonough, and I came up with a list of the top five coaches we'd like to have a beer with after a game, win or lose. After years of working together, and decades upon decades of combined years around the game, we had some very strong opinions about players, coaches, and teams, and we weren't shy about sharing those opinions with each other. We would update our "beer summit" list, and debate it, usually over our own beers. It was difficult to limit the list to five, and the real debate was reached at the final two spots. The No. 1 spot, however, was never up for reasonable debate, and never changed. In fact, it was never seriously argued.

The clear No. 1 coach on that list was Villanova's Jay Wright. It wasn't really a close call.

I first came to know Jay Wright when he was the head coach at Hofstra in the late 1990s. A former colleague of mine, current Notre Dame head coach Mike Brey, was the coach at rival Delaware, and told me that I should get to know Wright, because he was the real deal, and he could really coach. On Brey's advice, I started watching Hofstra closely in 1999 when Wright guided the Pride to the NIT, and then two straight NCAA Tournament bids. In March 2001, I decided to take a busman's holiday to see Hoftsra play UCLA in the NCAA Tournament in Greensboro, and I was sold. Brey was right—Jay Wright was, indeed, the real deal.

Hofstra lost to UCLA that day in Greensboro, in a game that Hofstra could have won. After the game, Wright was gracious, completely in control of his emotions, and made sure that every person in his charge had exactly what they needed, physically and emotionally. In short, you could tell that Wright gets it.

Wright is a Philly guy, and from his Hofstra success, he was able to go back home to Villanova as the Wildcats' head coach. In his first few years back on the Main Line, Wright was in Charlotte, North Carolina, for a Villanova alumni event. Former Philadelphia 76er Mike Gminski and I decided to go to the event to support him. The event was far less of a celebratory welcome than Wright gets from Villanova fans today, so Gminski and I took Wright to dinner afterward. At an Italian restaurant (after all, Wright is still a Rollie Massimino disciple), he shared with us the difficulties of laying down the right foundation, and wondered whether he would be allowed enough time. Gminski and I both echoed the same things to Wright—he reminded us of Mike Krzyzewski in his first few years at Duke, and we told him we believed he would not only get it rolling, but he would take his program to multiple Final Fours during his career. Wright appreciated the support and kind words, but also told us that he was coaching in Philly, and Philly fans don't really care what other people think. They want to see it for themselves. Now.

Even though Villanova is just outside of Philadelphia, it's still a Philly team. I'm not from Philadelphia, but I have always believed that Philly fans get a bad rap. You boo Santa Claus one time, and you're misunderstood for life! Philly fans are not just good, Philly fans are great. They have high expectations, but I don't know of any great fan base that does not. Philly fans are passionate, gritty, engaged, and loud. Philly fans want you to be one of them, and they don't just want you to play hard, they want you to fight. They will stay with you until the bitter end as long as you fight until the end. They want you to be one of them.

Jay Wright is all Philly. He may look Madison Avenue in his suits tailored by a guy named Gabriel D'Annunzio, but he is old-school Philly. Wright is laser-focused on winning, but very aware of the feelings and expectations of those around him. Philly fans value that. Wright is as upset and bothered after a loss as any competitor, yet he will not allow that competitive fire to burn those around him. Philly fans respect that. Everybody can be Mr. Wonderful after a win. Jay Wright is Mr. Wonderful to everyone after a win or a loss. That is uncommon, and Philly fans get that about Wright. He can operate just as effectively in a board room as in a locker room, and he makes everyone feel important, from the CEO to the bus driver. Philly fans grasp that, and appreciate it. Wright is confident without being overconfident. When Kris Jenkins let the winning jumper go against North Carolina, Wright could be seen saying, "Bang." Wright will tell you that he often does that whenever he sees a player step up and take the right shot with confidence. On the flip side, when an opponent takes a similar shot that might hurt the Wildcats, he will say, "No way." Wright insists there was nothing special or unusual about his saying "Bang," and I believe him. But it's still pretty damn cool. What player wouldn't want his coach saying "Bang" when they pull the trigger on a big shot?

I'm not naïve. I know that, in Philadelphia, there will always be tension and some bad blood among the old Philly rivals, and that will never go away. That is among the things that make Philly basketball great. But even the most hardened Philly rival had to love seeing Villanova fight to the end against the toughest draw in the NCAA Tournament, and come out on top. It was, in a word, remarkable.

Most people will tell you that Jay Wright hasn't changed at all over the years. Well, I beg to differ. He has changed—he has gotten better and better. In the last three years culminating in the 2016 national championship, Villanova is 97–13, winning more games over that period than any other team in the nation. But Wright is still striving for more, for sustained excellence. The Big East has changed, and things are much harder. Recruiting is harder. Getting exposure is harder. Winning is harder. Yet, Wright gets better. His core values have not changed, and they won't change after the 2016 national championship. But he's a better coach today than he was two years ago, and he will be better than ever next year. After the national championship, Wright was aggressive about learning how best to handle it. He sought out advice from Mike Krzyzewski, Jim Boeheim, Gregg Popovich, and others. Jay Wright is striving to get better, even after his crowning achievement. Philly fans will absolutely love that.

And every sports fan will love this book by Dana O'Neil. I am so glad that Dana is writing this book on Villanova and its title season. She has as much in-depth knowledge of Villanova, Wright, and their journey since his hiring as anyone, and there is nobody's work I trust more than Dana's. I know that when I read her, I will learn something

I didn't know. Dana knows the game, and understands the people in the game.

One thing I have learned about teams and championship seasons is that you may be there for every team meal, bus ride, plane ride, practice, and game, but you don't know every story within the team. Even the Villanova players and coaches will read Dana's book and learn details about their season that even they didn't know. The Wildcats were "all in" on this journey, and really seemed not to mind what people said or thought along the way. So many of us "experts" picked against the Wildcats, but they didn't seem to care. In fact, they didn't seem to listen. They just fought. And they just won.

Villanova just finished a historic ride, and Dana O'Neil is the perfect writer to take us inside that ride. Hang on, it's going to be fun to relive it all. Enjoy it!

—Jay Bilas

Jay Bilas, known for his extensive knowledge of men's basketball and insightful analysis about the sports industry, joined ESPN in 1995. He is featured on ESPN's game and studio coverage, and calls the top men's college basketball games involving the nation's marquee teams and conferences. He also writes for ESPN.com, and contributes to SportsCenter *and* ESPN Radio. Sports Illustrated *has twice named him the best analyst in college basketball.*

Prologue

Daniel Ochefu lay on his left side, a trail of sweat marking his path across the floor. He had dived for the ball but missed, and so, out of the play and out of the action, he quickly rolled over on his back, sat up, and looked at the basket.

Ryan Arcidiacono barely had enough time to find his footing. He had sailed in after Ochefu, flying out from the free-throw line to distract the shooter, his arms stretched over his head. His efforts, too, were in vain, and so he skip-stepped, turned, and looked in the same direction as Ochefu, at the basket.

So they saw it. The two Villanova captains saw North Carolina's Marcus Paige, his legs splayed as if he were riding a bicycle, jump and double-clutch a circus three-point shot from the wing.

They saw the ball arcing toward the net and eventually slipping through it. They heard the celebratory pandemonium of the North Carolina fans and they felt the panic from the Villanova faithful.

And they didn't flinch.

"It's a situation we practice literally every single day in practice, so we knew what was going to happen," Arcidiacono said. "Honestly, as soon as he scored, I think we were envisioning the play already."

The play is appropriately called "Nova," appropriate because it is more than a series of erasable Xs and Os on a whiteboard. It represents what this Villanova team is, what head coach Jay Wright reconfigured his Villanova program to be. To execute Nova properly, players need to be disciplined in their roles yet confident in their ability to adjust on the fly.

The play, like the program, is as much about trust as it is execution, about doing the little things right to produce big results.

Since he arrived on campus in 2001, that's the sort of team Wright always wanted to coach. That, however, is not always who Villanova was. Seven years earlier, the Wildcats made it to the Final Four—point guard Scottie Reynolds using a different version of Nova to score a buzzer beater in the regional final against Pittsburgh to get them there—but rather than continue to build on its sturdy base, the program's foundation began to crumble.

A combination of bad recruiting decisions and lousy execution led to a slow slide that ended in a 13–19 record nadir in 2012.

At the same time, the Big East, Villanova's conference home for more than three decades, started to fall apart, too. Realignment left the league ripe for poaching and soon, teams including cornerstone programs such as Syracuse and Pittsburgh, were headed out to greener pastures—greener, at least, on the gridiron, to satiate all-mighty football.

Out of such a shaky introduction, Ochefu and Arcidiacono, along with three walk-ons, helped reconstruct Villanova. The Redemption Class, they called themselves, determined to write a different future for the program. And almost immediately, they did. Villanova would go from 13–19 to 20–14 in their freshman season.

But then along came a new level of failure. Villanova could win in the regular season, but not in the postseason, awarded a high seed in the NCAA Tournament only to be ousted in the first weekend for three consecutive years. Critics understandably eyed a roster devoid of NBA lottery picks, from a league that still hadn't entirely reshaped its identity, and deemed Villanova a nice, plucky little Catholic school that really couldn't stand toe-to-toe with the big boys.

Along came the 2016 season, a magical ride that saw the Wildcats lose but four regular-season games and not just dump the NCAA Tournament monkey on their back; they heaved it out of sight.

For five NCAA Tournament games, Villanova essentially strung together a series of Novas, of one flawlessly executed yet instinctively ad-libbed play after another. The Wildcats were so good, ousting opponents by an average of 24.5 points per game, that it all seemed effortless. In the national semifinal, Villanova sent Oklahoma and national player of the year Buddy Hield into full retreat, winning by a Final Four record 44 points and leaving the usually ebullient Hield silently hiding beneath a towel as the final seconds ticked away.

On the Monday night of the title game, Villanova continued to work its magic, turning a six-point deficit into a 10-point lead in a mere 10 minutes. The Wildcats were more fearless than fancy, boldly taking the ball to the rim against North Carolina's size, doubling down defensively to stop the Tar Heels' vaunted transition game.

Villanova was Nova.

And then it all went wrong. The hard work slipped away in a blink, yet felt like the slow and steady pressure of a vice clamping down on Villanova's season.

It started with an errant pass, with Arcidiacono, a four-year captain, slinging one to Ochefu that the big man couldn't handle. It was the senior's first turnover of the game, just his eighth of the entire NCAA Tournament. At the time it seemed like a silly mistake, not the beginning of a crisis. From the sideline, Wright yelled, "Use a bounce pass."

Still, with 4:42 left to play, Villanova held a comfortable 67–59 lead.

A little more than two minutes later, the situation was anything but comfortable. North Carolina's big men, stymied for most of the game by the quicker and deceptively strong Wildcats, finally announced themselves. Brice Johnson and Isaiah Hicks blocked two shots and altered two more, and when Kris Jenkins, arguably the Wildcats' best shooter, stepped to the free-throw line for a one-and-one opportunity, the Wildcats' lead was down to 69–64.

Jenkins missed.

"I just bricked it," Jenkins said with a chuckle.

"I had never seen him do that in three years," Arcidiacono said. "He's such a good shooter and for him to miss is so uncharacteristic. I said to him, 'Hey, don't get nervous on me now, bro.' And he just looked at me and said, 'I got you.'"

Just 2:20 remained on the clock.

The Villanova players insisted then and reaffirmed later that they weren't nervous or feeling any pressure. They always expected North Carolina to make a run and were hardly surprised when the final push came. Yet everything that the Wildcats had avoided in much of the tournament—making foolish mistakes, forcing bad shots, playing tight—started to happen at once, and what seemed like a certain march to a national title began to unravel string by string. After Jenkins missed a free throw, Josh Hart, a 75 percent shooter at the line, went only 1-of-2.

The Cats, who had played so aggressively all season and marched through the tournament with an almost merciless ability to keep their foot to the throttle, backed off. They tried to drain the shot clock on each possession, forcing last-second heaves instead of taking what was available to them.

"In the second half, you know, I looked at Arch, I looked at myself, and said, 'Yeah, we got to pick it up,'" Ochefu said.

There comes a point in every close game when you can almost feel the momentum in the building shift, abandoning one bench and taking a seat on another. In the national championship game, that moment came with 90 seconds left to play. Paige, dogged all season by a shooting slump that cost him any shot at national honors, took an inbounds pass in the corner directly in front of his bench, rose up, and drained a three-pointer. In the panicked rush to call a timeout, North Carolina coach Roy Williams, hobbling around all season on a knee that would need to be replaced, slipped and had to limp down his bench to signal for the break.

Paige's shot cut Villanova's lead to 70–67.

In the huddle, Williams set up a trap and when play restarted, Joel Berry and Paige executed it to perfection. They caught an unsuspecting Arcidiacono just as he crossed midcourt. Again Arcidiacono tried to get the ball to Ochefu. Except the pass was too high and too long and sailed out of bounds.

This time Wright put his hands on his hips, turned away from the action, and said nothing.

Eight seconds later, Johnson banked in a hook shot, and as Villanova headed to the bench for a timeout with one minute to play, the Wildcats' lead was down to one, 70–69.

"When we took the 10-point lead, given how the game had gone up to that point, we never figured we'd get a double-digit lead," associate head coach Baker Dunleavy said. "We figured this is going to be one of those games that comes down to the wire, so I don't think we were rattled."

Phil Booth, the unsung hero of this game for Villanova, pushed the lead back to three when he sank two free throws. Only a sophomore, Booth would finish with 20 points and miss just one shot from the floor, and when Villanova desperately needed a big play, he came up with it. Booth drove to the right side of the lane, trailed by Hicks, and though he slipped trying to launch for his jumper, he wisely leaned into Hicks to draw the foul. With 35.7 seconds remaining, Villanova led 72–69.

But Paige, too, was gunning for a spot as end-game hero. When the 6-foot-3 senior wrested a rebound out of Hart's hands and connected on a circus up-and-over layup amid a forest of much bigger men, he earned more than a few votes. North Carolina was back to within one with 23 seconds left.

Villanova managed to bleed 10 seconds off the game clock before Johnson fouled Hart. The junior sunk both free throws, giving Villanova a 74–71 cushion with 13.5 seconds left to play.

Which leads us to the sprawled-out Ochefu and the backward-looking Arcidiacono.

The two leaders of the Redemption Class not only redeemed the Wildcats; they came to symbolize what Wright wanted Villanova to be—smart and tough, selfless and humble. Along the way, they also helped the Big East resurrect itself from the ashes of realignment, and gave the league an identity.

They are Villanova.

They are Nova.

And there they were, helpless as Berry pushed the ball across mid-court before dishing it to his right, to Paige.

"My instinct kicked in right away to throw the ball to Brice right under the basket," Paige said. "That's why I hesitated with the ball when I jumped. Obviously, we needed three."

Paige managed to sidestep the diving Ochefu, who tried to intercept the pass from Berry, but as Paige rose up for his shot, Arcidiacono flashed in his face. It was just enough interference to force Paige into a crazy-looking, helter-skelter, off-balance three-point shot, a shot that became a guaranteed "One Shining Moment" instant classic as soon as it swished through the net, tying the score with 4.7 seconds left to play.

Paige pumped his fist once as his bench erupted. Williams stalked the sideline, not smiling but clapping his hands and shouting, "Get a stop, get a stop."

In the stands just behind the North Carolina bench, Michael Jordan, the greatest Tar Heel of them all, raised his hands above his head triumphantly while the Villanova faithful put their hands over their eyes and mouthed, "Oh my God."

In the stands across from the Villanova bench, Arcidiacono's father, Joe, accepted what he figured was his son's inevitable fate.

"Paige hits that crazy shot and I go, 'No, this is how it's supposed to end. We're the little tank engine that can. It's almost there. I think we can, I think we can, but no,'" Joe Arcidiacono said. "I'm kind of laughing, going, 'Well, that's why they're Carolina, right?'"

In the midst of the mayhem, Wright calmly called for a timeout and then the most amazing thing of all happened, more amazing even than Paige's miraculous shot.

Their season on the brink, their title slipping away, the Wildcats sprinted to the huddle. They didn't shuffle. Their heads were up, not hangdog. They looked their coach in the eye.

"I thought Paige's shot was unbelievable, but I also knew we had somewhat of a chance with 4.7 seconds left," Jenkins said. "So when he made that shot, Coach called the timeout and it was just attitude. Everyone is engaged, looking at Coach, waiting for him to set the play."

Jay Wright didn't have to call a play.

"We all knew," Arcidiacono said. "We were running Nova."

The Villanova players gathered round like they always do, a tight circle surrounding Jay Wright. Ryan Arcidiacono sat directly across from his coach; Kris Jenkins was at Wright's left elbow. Wright scribbled a few things on his whiteboard and everyone listened intently.

Seconds earlier North Carolina's Marcus Paige had connected on a circus three-point shot to tie the score at 74–74. Only 4.7 seconds remained for Villanova to win the national championship or settle for overtime. NRG Stadium practically buzzed with energy. At their courtside seats, reporters frantically rewrote their deadline stories. In the stands, even all the way up to the nether reaches of the dome, fans stood on their feet, too amazed at what just happened, too nervous to watch the end.

Yet that Villanova huddle, the one place that should have been frantic and chaotic, was an oasis of calm. No one spoke over each other or screamed. Really no one, aside from Wright, said a word. Instead, every player, assistant coach, and even manager stared intently as the coach began to speak.

How did the Wildcats, prepping for the biggest possession of the college basketball season, stay so relaxed?

Simple.

Jay Wright taught them.

When he first arrived on the Villanova campus in 2001, Wright introduced his players to Attitude Club. Admission is neither free nor open to everyone. Players earn their way into the exclusive group by leaving skid marks on the floor diving for a loose ball, bruising their backside taking a charge, stretching for an extra inch in their vertical leap to tap back a rebound, or any of a myriad of hustle plays that don't show up in a box score. Every time the Wildcats compete, a staff member charts attitude points and a winner is declared after each practice, each game, and at the end of the season. Leading in attitude points is more coveted than leading the team in scoring.

To Wright—and now by extension to his players—attitude, not points, wins games. How a player prepares himself and supports his teammates, how he carries himself in victory, in defeat, and especially in the most difficult times, is the difference between winning and losing.

And so when the Wildcats circled up for the last huddle of the 2015–16 season, even with just 4.7 seconds left to cover 94 feet of open floor, they were ready.

"It was like, 'Okay, this is what we've been working toward.' Not the national championship itself, but what we call preparing for the most difficult situation," said associate head coach Baker Dunleavy. "Everyone's mentality was, 'Okay, I'm not going to be the one that loses his cool. I know what my teammates are thinking, what my coaches are thinking, so I'm going to fall in line.' As crazy as it sounds, we almost practice for it."

The all-time Attitude Club champion?

That would be Jay Wright. People love to talk about Wright's looks and menswear finery—his suits even have their own Twitter handle, @JayWrightsSuit. While other coaches wrestle with neckties that appear to be choking them, or give in to shirttails that refuse to stay tucked, Wright is permanently pressed. President Barack Obama even referred to Wright as the "George Clooney of coaches." From his pocket square tucked neatly in his suit pocket to his hair coiffed to perfection, he is the personification of the old Gillette advertisement—"Never let 'em see you sweat."

The motto fits more than his appearance. It suits his demeanor as well. Wright is a fierce competitor. Players, friends, and fellow coaches love nothing more than to debunk the theory that Wright is as easygoing as his pleasant personality might suggest. But as he's grown as a coach, he's developed an almost inverse reaction to stress—the tighter and tougher the situation, the more relaxed he is.

So when Wright sat down to illustrate the Wildcats' final play—a play everyone already knew—what he said wasn't important. It was how he delivered the message.

"Calm, cool, and collected, that's him to a tee," said Speedy Claxton, who played for Wright at Hofstra. "His teams feed off of that. You play the way he is."

Mike Mikulski, Wright's best friend since childhood, remembers a similar huddle some 40 years ago.

During a timeout, Mike Holland, the Council Rock High School boys basketball coach, gathered his players around in the midst of a tight game and drew up a play. The boys listened intently, understood what was being asked of them, and then headed on to the court.

Except before the referee whistled to begin play, one of the boys called his teammates together. There, without a clipboard—and more, without his coach's knowledge or consent—Jay Wright changed the play.

"And here's the thing," Mikulski said. "Everyone fell in line. We changed the play."

Understandably furious afterward, Holland screeched at Wright to never upstage him like that again, reminding him that the play he designed would have worked. Wright smirked.

"Mine did, too," he said.

"I said he was competitive. I never said he was easy," Mikulski laughed, recalling the story.

There are more signs like that, ones that with hindsight seem to predestine Jay Wright to becoming a head coach. He was a hardworking and overachieving first-born child; the son of a fundamentals-first father and a gregarious mother; academically and athletically gifted; voted best dressed and best looking, yet never stand-offish; a starter one year and a bench player the next, all traits that serve a coach well.

But Jay Wright did not grow up with a grand plan. He loved Villanova basketball as a kid, but never once told his buddies he wished he could coach there. He starred at basketball, and yet didn't envision spending his life on a court.

He was merely driven and confident, even if he didn't always know exactly where he was headed.

"Jay just did stuff and it never dawned on him that it might fail," Mikulski said.

Even today, Wright has a casualness about his success. Days after winning the national championship, he sat in his office trying to understand what had happened. He couldn't comprehend it—not just in the sense that he was amazed by the exciting finish of the game itself. He couldn't grasp what it all meant—for Villanova, for basketball, and especially for him.

"I just feel like we won a big game," he said. "You know, you win a big game, people in the media call you for a few days. That's what this feels like. When someone says that we won a national championship or we're national champions, it doesn't seem real."

Those who know him well say he's always been like that, consumed with the goal of winning but not drunk on the aftermath of glory. That's unusual, especially in the profession that Wright has chosen.

College basketball, unlike the NBA, is ruled by its coaches. The athletes move on after a quick stopover on campus. Coaches stick around. If they are good, they become the face of a program. If they are great, they become icons. Success typically equals bigger salaries, more demands, and less reality.

Wright isn't a fan of that exchange.

When he first arrived at Villanova, he stood on tabletops in the cafeteria, desperate to drum up interest in the program. Fifteen years later, he still loves to ride around campus in a golf cart, chatting up students, even stopping to purchase a T-shirt from the women's soccer players selling them at a table.

Since the national championship game, he has talked hoops with the president of the United States, but says he most looks forward to a few days off at his house on the Jersey Shore.

"My wife, when she first met him was like, 'Oh God, right. Look at him,'" said Wright's former assistant Joe Jones. "After a month of being around him, we were going home after an event and she looked at me and says, 'You're 100 percent right. He's as nice and as good as you said.' I was stunned. I said, 'You questioned that?' She said, 'Totally.'"

It's a common mistake. If Wright has battled anything throughout his career it is the misconception that, because he looks a certain way, he must be a certain way. "Tailored suits, million-dollar smile, and the personality, but what people fail to see is the depth," said Father Rob Hagan, an associate athletic director who goes by Father Rob and a regular on Villanova's bench.

In some people that has understandably cultivated envy. Even Wright's younger brother, Derek, said he sat him down for a heart-to-heart a few years ago explaining that, as a basketball coach himself, sometimes it was hard to compete with the image of Jay Wright.

"He was like, 'Wow, really?'" said Derek, the head coach at Council Rock South High School, and younger than Wright by 13 years. "He never thought of it that way. But I explained how it was making me feel inadequate and he totally understood."

In others, Wright's appearance has fostered doubts. Early in his career plenty of people thought he was nothing but an empty head in a pretty suit, that he'd be overmatched when he went toe-to-toe with the real leaders of the game.

The truth? As of the end of the 2015–16 season, against Syracuse head coach Jim Boehiem, Wright is 12–9. Against Duke coach Mike Krzyzewski, he's 1–0. Against Louisville's Rick Pitino, he's 6–5.

Those coaches are all in the Hall of Fame.

As for Wright?

"He doesn't care," Jones said. "He's always been above all of that."

So where does such confidence, such an ease in oneself, come from?

"You know that saying, 'raised right'?" Mikulski said. "Well, he was raised right."

Quintessential baby boomers who grew up in northeast Philadelphia but raised their family in the suburbs, Jerry and Judy Wright taught their kids to work hard but dream big. Jerry—Big Jer, to the neighborhood kids—worked as a power tools salesman and spent his evenings coaching the boys in Little League. He believed in teaching fundamentals but also delivered one common refrain to every group he coached—any team is only as good as its weakest player. Consequently, Big Jer made sure there was no such thing as a weak player, developing every kid to his fullest potential.

The strategy worked. As 10-year-olds, the Larks finished 18–3, losing the championship after poor Artie Gable, who Wright recalls as a great kid and a terrific lefty pitcher, failed to tag up at second base, negating a would-be sacrifice fly on the next play. A year later, they avenged Gable's mistake, winning the league championship.

Big Jer was friendly, if a bit more stoic with his emotions.

Judy, meantime, was the yin to her husband's yang. A homemaker, she made a home that was open to everyone. Gregarious, tall, pretty, and always impeccably dressed, Judy has never met a stranger—sometimes to her kid's embarrassment.

"I didn't appreciate it then, but now I see how his parents were very progressive," Mikulski said. "They were really good at fostering confidence. They weren't restrictive. My mom was the typical Italian mother. She was a lunatic, militant. His parents, they certainly disciplined their kids, but they gave them a lot of rope."

"The Golden Child," his siblings teasingly call the always overachieving Wright. If the neighborhood kids played basketball in the driveway until 10:00 PM, Wright would stay out until 11:30, working on his shot. When it was time to choose up sides for a game, he was always one of—if not the—first chosen. Academically, he was part of the school's gifted program. Athletically, he was good enough to be a quarterback on the football team, and a shortstop on the baseball team had he not elected to concentrate on basketball.

Living up to such high standards can, however, exact a toll. Wright never said as much, but his brother sensed it. Wright can be consumed by doing things well, relentlessly pursuing perfection to the exclusion of everything else.

"Maybe it's the Protestant in us, or the northwestern European heritage, but it's almost like you can be so concerned about doing the right thing and what you should do, you don't even necessarily enjoy the moments as they happen," Derek said. "Showing your vulnerability, that's a limit for all of us sometimes."

Wright compensated by never being vulnerable, plastering a smile on his face and soldiering forward.

Though he didn't intend to be a coach early on, Wright had plenty of people to model himself after. There was Big Jer, of course, but Wright also grew up in the heyday of Philadelphia's Big 5 basketball tradition. Harry Litwack, Jack Kraft, and Chuck Daly were among the great coaches to prowl the sidelines back when Saint Joseph's, Temple, Penn, La Salle, and Villanova played a full round-robin schedule.

The basketball itself was even better. Every City Series game was staged at the historic Palestra, often as double-headers. In 1979, the same year that Wright would graduate from Council Rock High School, the University of Pennsylvania would reach the Final Four.

But Villanova was Wright's favorite team.

"I know people today say that's all BS," Mikulski said. "It's not BS. That's who he rooted for."

When he wasn't watching games, Wright was playing. In high school, he'd jump in his first car, a Capri, and drive to the Sonny Hill League, the renowned basketball summer league in North Philadelphia. Even there, a suburban small fish in the inner-city big pond, he made friends. He'd come home and persuade his buddies to head outside of their comfy suburban confines for pickup games.

Naturally, they'd go.

A talented, long-armed guard, Wright earned some college attention, opting to attend Bucknell University, a small school with rigorous academics about three hours west of Philadelphia.

Wright and his buddies back home figured he'd continue on as always, sliding right in with the team's roster. But being the star at Council Rock isn't quite the same as being a college athlete. Even at Bucknell, a school a few rungs removed from the sport's upper echelon, Wright soon learned that lesson. In letters to Mikulski, who attended La Salle, Wright told his friend about the talented players on the Bison roster, guys such as Albert Leslie, who would go on to become a second-round NBA pick. Wright admitted to being a little overwhelmed and for the first time feeling a little less than confident.

That, however, didn't stop him from bringing the same intensity to the college courts as he did to his own driveway. Pat Flannery was a senior when Wright arrived on campus. He immediately took a liking to the new kid and Wright long has called Flannery one of his mentors. The first time Flannery saw Wright play—in a pickup game against his future teammates—he knew Bucknell had found a competitor.

"He tried to challenge the score and calls with a group of pretty good upperclassmen," Flannery said.

Wright earned a starting spot as a junior, but as the roster continued to improve, his playing time diminished. By his senior year he was coming off the bench, a humbling experience for a kid who'd always been picked first, and one he understandably didn't enjoy. Years later, as he grew into a coach, Wright often recalled his own college experience. He learned not only the value of a good bench, but also the importance of making certain that players outside the starting lineup felt as vital as the ones leading the team in scoring.

It was like he was living his father's old motto—a team is only as good as its weakest link.

Like a lot of new college graduates, Wright, who majored in economics and sociology, wasn't quite sure what to do with himself after he graduated from Bucknell. He landed a marketing gig with the Philadelphia Stars, the local United States Football League team.

From an office in the bowels of the old Veterans Stadium, he'd try to sell tickets to an audience (including his own father) that had an allegiance to just one football team—the Philadelphia Eagles. Still, Wright made cold calls and occasionally stumped at local town halls for publicity events. Sometimes he'd be joined by another marketing rep, a woman by the name of Patty Reilly. A recent Villanova graduate and former cheerleader there, she worked in the same department as Wright and doubled as a Stars cheerleader.

Once, as everyone who loves to share embarrassing stories about Wright is only too happy to tell, Wright even doubled as the team mascot. The man meant to don the furry gold costume failed to show, so Wright plopped the overstuffed head on his shoulders and peddled his wares to commuters making their way through 30th Street Station, Philadelphia's busy train hub.

"That's the real story about how he got his start," Flannery said.

Fate—or is it fortune?—has a way of insinuating itself into life, detouring a plan from one trail and onto another. For Wright, fate came in the form of Flannery, his good-natured college pal. Flannery had gone directly from playing basketball to coaching, sitting on the bench at his alma mater in Wright's final two seasons before moving on to Drexel. He'd been offered an assistant's gig at Rochester, a Division III school, but decided he liked his Drexel job more.

So, he recommended Wright for the Rochester position. At the time, Wright's basketball experience included a few turns as a camp counselor back home in Bucks County.

"From that first pickup game, we loved him from then on," Flannery said. "Jay was always into hoops and we knew basketball would be in some aspect of his future."

Wright took the gig, kissed a future in sales good-bye, and started peddling Rochester as vigorously as he'd sold the Stars.

Flannery not only set Wright up with his first job; he partnered him with a terrific head coach in Mike Neer. When he retired in 2014, Neer had amassed a 629–346 record in 37 years as a head coach, making him one of fewer than 100 coaches in history to win more than 600 games.

But being an assistant coach in Division III isn't exactly a glamorous gig. Wright wore many hats in his days at Rochester, including running the intramural programs and coaching the junior varsity team.

It was that intramural gig, in fact, that tore Wright away from the first Final Four he'd ever attended. The championship weekend doubles as the National Association of Basketball Coaches convention, so Wright was thrilled when he got to go to Lexington, Kentucky. He was able to stay for the semifinals but when the championship game tipped off, he was in the home of the Rochester soccer coach, sitting on the floor, watching the television.

The year was 1985; the champion, Villanova.

"The guys who played floor hockey didn't really care about the national championship game," Wright later recalled when telling the story.

Even missing his favorite childhood team win a title didn't sour Wright on Rochester or coaching. He loved it. When the coaching bug bites, it rarely lets go, infecting people with a passion that sends them on a lifelong, often nomadic, trail.

Wright may not have been seeking a coaching career but when it found him, it was a match made in hoops heaven.

Wright is a natural fidgeter who prefers activities—kayaking, bodysurfing, tennis—to actually sitting on his beloved Jersey Shore beaches, the sort who feeds off the adrenaline-rush, no-sleep lifestyle that coaching often demands. Derek Wright remembered one morning when his brother left the house after just a two- or three-hour visit for a recruiting trip.

It was Christmas morning.

"And he was making nothing, but he loved it," Derek said.

So when, two years after he took the Rochester job on a lark, he had a chance to join Flannery as an assistant at Drexel, Wright jumped at the chance. He could go back home.

Philadelphia is nothing if not provincial. Everyone seemingly knows everyone, or knows a guy who knows a guy. The basketball community there is even more tight-knit. Coaches and players want nothing more than to beat their city rivals during the year, but then work together in the off-season regularly. So in the summers, during his downtime at Drexel, Wright spent his time counseling at Villanova's camps.

Hot off of that national championship, the Wildcats were the biggest college story in town and head coach Rollie Massimino their king. The popular paisan took a liking to Wright, and the following year hired him to his staff.

Wright spent five seasons on the Main Line, sitting on the bench of the team he grew up idolizing. Close to home, where his parents could come and watch their son work, it was perfect.

And, it turns out, too good to be true, or at least too good to last. In 1991, after Massimino cited an expanded Big East schedule and NCAA rules that mandated each team play only 27 games, he asked that Villanova be allowed to reduce the number of Big 5 games it played. It was the first crack in what would become a Big 5 earthquake. The City Series continued but as a poor man's version, with each school playing just two other Philly opponents.

The breakup of the Big 5 certainly wasn't Massimino's fault, but he delivered the first blow. Forget that Villanova's demands were different than the other four schools. Folks viewed Villanova as the snooty school outside the city limits and vilified Massimino. He was the villain who killed the Philadelphia tradition.

That, coupled with diminishing returns on the court after the 1985 national championship, led the coach to first voice his displeasure and frustration with his job, and later, seek opportunities elsewhere. When UNLV, desperate to revamp its image after the NCAA-stained tenure of renegade coach Jerry Tarkanian, called, he jumped. And Massimino took his staff with him.

Wright didn't exactly want to go to. Just a year earlier, he'd married his onetime Philadelphia Stars marketing partner, Patty Reilly. But his loyalty to Massimino was strong.

So the East Coast guy relocated and tried to make his way in the desert. Wright's first two children, Taylor and Colin, were born in Vegas. The Wrights, in fact, happened upon the name Colin because of a local radio host in town—Colin Cowherd, now a national radio and TV personality for Fox Sports.

Two years later, in 1994, Massimino rewarded Wright for his loyalty, recommending him for the head coaching job at Hofstra. On April 14 of that year, Wright was introduced at Hofstra. He was 33, and his team was terrible. The Pride (then called the Flying Dutchmen) was in its 21st season as a Division I basketball program. In 17 of those years, Hofstra finished below .500. The school's NCAA Tournament legacy consisted of a whopping two appearances, one in 1976 and one in 1977. To say the students were apathetic about their team would imply they knew a team even existed.

"He'd have me go to these meetings with spirit groups—cheerleaders, baton twirlers—trying to get them enthused," said Jones, who joined Wright on his staff that first year. "The day of the game, he'd be at the Dunkin Donuts handing out tickets."

There are overnight success stories in coaching. Wright's tenure at Hofstra was not one of them. In his first two years at the helm, Wright won 19 games combined, just 10 in the America East Conference. Despite Wright's near begging, nobody came to the games.

The turnaround came in 1996 when Wright offered a scholarship to a kid by the name of Craig Claxton. Everyone called him "Speedy."

Claxton grew up in Hempstead, New York, on Long Island, but every day he'd make the 45-minute commute to New York City so he could play at Christ the King High School, a basketball powerhouse. Lamar Odom, once the NBA Sixth Man of the Year and now famous as the former husband of reality star Khloe Kardashian, was one of his teammates.

Claxton was small—just 5-feet-11—so as he moved through high school, most of the power colleges weren't terribly interested in recruiting him. Even the New York schools paid Claxton little mind.

Except for Hofstra.

Every time Claxton played in a game or in a tournament, one of the Hofstra coaches was in the stands. In the days before social media, cell phones, and texting, Wright sent Claxton a handwritten note almost every day.

"I kept seeing him, seeing him. He was constantly in my face," Claxton said of Wright.

Before his senior year, Claxton committed to Hofstra but per NCAA rules, a verbal commitment isn't binding. Players aren't obligated to attend a school until they sign letters of intent in their senior years. In other words, if he chose to, Claxton could change his mind.

And then Claxton had one of those dream senior seasons. Local newspapers started calling Claxton the most exciting player in New

York City, suddenly discovering the small guard with a big game. Just as quickly the same big schools—including St. John's—that wanted nothing to do with Claxton a year earlier started wooing him.

He wouldn't budge. Being comfortable, he said, was more important than some big-name school, and Wright made him comfortable.

He arrived at Hofstra in the fall of 1996.

After one workout, he was ready to leave.

Perhaps one of the greatest misconceptions about Wright is that he's too nice to be tough. Publicly he comes across as so likable, so perennially upbeat, that people assume he's a pushover.

"Oh no, he's a competitive you-know-what," Mikulski said.

Before his players love him, in fact, most of them hate him, realizing almost immediately that the friendly coach they came to know during their recruitment is actually both Jekyll and Hyde. His practices are not for the meek; Wright's suggestions and corrections are usually laced with a large dose of impatience, sneer, and a good dose of R-rated language.

"Don't even get me started," said Claxton, now an assistant coach at his alma mater. "Totally different person on the court. First thing I realized was, 'Whoa, this is not the man who recruited me.' Let's just say it was a long freshman year."

To Wright, not hustling is a sin and not working hard on defense a mortal sin. Most everyone who has played for Wright has a freshman-season horror story, one where they questioned their own abilities because of his demands. Daniel Ochefu's freshman year was not terribly unlike Claxton's. He remembered one period, after a particularly lousy run of losing. School was closed for winter break, but the Wildcats were on campus and Wright, furious and disgusted with their play, worked them relentlessly.

Every morning the players would wake before dawn and trudge through the snow to the gym. Hours later, they'd walk back in the same stinging cold and snow to the dorm, too exhausted to even spend time with one another.

"It was like boot camp," Ochefu said. "I think halfway through that week, I was like, 'I don't know if I can keep up with this. Is this what I want to do?' It was awful."

Wright doesn't limit his competitive edge to his players, either. His adult friends, like his childhood friends, have encountered the fierce competitor who can't help but try to win every battle. Jones recalled some pickup basketball games that turned ferocious.

"He ripped my shoulder off one time," he said. "There was a loose ball, and I don't know if I dove for it—I might have leaned over. He dove for it and my hand was under the ball. He ripped the ball so freaking hard, I was hurt."

Coaches today often lament that they can't treat players the same way they used to, that to demand too much of them is to risk losing them, and to risk losing them is to risk losing a job. Increased salaries have raised expectations so much that coaches can ill afford to alienate the athletes who essentially hold the keys to their success or failure.

Wright has tried hard not to make that exchange, not even for arguably the best player he has coached. Today, Kyle Lowry is an NBA All-Star and an Olympic gold medalist. At Villanova, he was an all-star pain in the neck. Tough on the court, he was hardheaded off of it, resistant to authority, challenging, and flat-out frustrating. He and Wright butted heads regularly. Lowry questioned everything, never satisfied with a simple "Because I told you to," as a response.

But rather than give in, Wright challenged Lowry right back. He'd send him to the sidelines for sprints if he misbehaved and tossed him out of practice regularly when his attitude didn't improve. He spent more hours than he cares to count in conversation—sometimes heated and sometimes threatening—trying to get Lowry to understand he wasn't going to cave in to his whims.

Rather than dismiss Wright or question his authority, Lowry welcomed the direction.

"He didn't promise me anything and I appreciated that," Lowry said. "So many people told me what I wanted to hear. He'd throw me out of practice, but every time I came back because I knew I needed it. I was going to be me, but I also knew I needed him and what he was doing for me."

The players who have survived Wright—and most have—tell a similar story, and once they emerge on the other side they, like Lowry, remain fiercely loyal to him. They often even come to understand why their coach demanded so much of them in the first place.

Claxton figured it out pretty quickly, seeing the results of his labor on the court. In his sophomore year, Hofstra enjoyed its first winning season in five years. A year later, the team earned a postseason berth with a bid to the National Invitation Tournament.

Finally, in Claxton's senior year, Hofstra won a total of 24 games, claimed the league championship, and earned a trip to the NCAA Tournament.

"He instills culture," Claxton said. "You have no choice but to fall in line, and once you fall in line, you carry that through your four years. Every freshman eventually will fall in line because that's how you win and everybody loves to win. I tell my guys now, the only way to win is to play hard."

Perhaps the only thing harder to do than succeeding once is doing it over and over. For Wright, the task was especially difficult after Claxton graduated. The same player once labeled too tiny for big-name schools was selected 20th overall in the NBA Draft on the merits of a college career that included 2,000 points and school records in both assists and steals.

But gifted with a returning lineup loaded with upperclassmen, Wright repeated his magic. Hofstra won two more games than the year before—26 in all—claimed another America East Conference crown, and earned a return ticket to the NCAA Tournament.

The success, coupled with Wright's engaging personality, turned the coach into the hottest commodity in his profession, especially on the East Coast where Wright's polished look and city-slick demeanor especially resonated.

Hofstra lost its final game of the season, a first-round NCAA Tournament game against UCLA, on March 15, 2001. Six days later, Rutgers fired embattled head coach Kevin Bannon. It didn't take long for Tom Mulcahy, Rutgers' athletic director at the time—and a Villanova graduate to boot—to turn his attention to Wright.

For Wright, Rutgers ticked all of the right boxes. He wouldn't have to move his family—daughter, Reilly, was born in 1998—too far. It was in a recruiting region he knew well and at the time, the Scarlet Knights were competing in the Big East, arguably the best basketball league in the country and a conference Wright grew up watching.

Negotiations, in fact, were so far along that at one point, Wright called Mikulski, his lifelong friend, to tell him he was headed to Rutgers.

"It was close, very close," Wright said.

The only last T to cross, in fact, was for Wright to sit down with the Rutgers chancellor. The meeting was scheduled for a Sunday.

Except, two days earlier, Villanova coach Steve Lappas took the UMass job. The parting between school and coach was awkward, if not altogether messy. Lappas technically left but there was a sense that he was getting out ahead of the firing squad. The Wildcats had done well under the former Massimino assistant but underperformed in the postseason, backing up a first-round exit in the 1999 NCAA Tournament with two NIT berths.

Villanova was anxious to get in on the Jay Wright sweepstakes.

"[Jay] was getting a lot of attention from other schools," said Vince Nicastro, who was the Villanova athletic director at the time. "He was very far down the path with Rutgers and we had to move pretty quickly to get his attention. Had we waited a day or two, he may not have been able to come back and look at Villanova."

Instead of meeting with the Rutgers chancellor, Wright sat down with Nicastro on that Sunday. Nicastro offered Wright the job on the spot.

"It was maybe two days later and he called me again and said, 'Okay, I'm not going to Rutgers,'" Mikulski said. "It was because it was Villanova. That was it for him."

It always has been it for Wright, from childhood until the present day.

He has been courted for other jobs, including cream-of-the-college-crop Kentucky, and his hometown NBA franchise, the Philadelphia 76ers. He has considered some more thoughtfully than others but he has never been close to leaving Villanova.

"People have to understand, Villanova is Jay's dream job," said his former assistant coach Billy Lange. "As much as it means to him personally, he also considers himself something of a steward of the program."

Wright also likes the rhythm of the school and the city.

Despite its rich college basketball history, Philadelphia is a pro sports town first, second, last, and always. Villanova can be 0–10 or 10–0 to start the season and the local media, including the vibrant talk-radio community, won't pay much attention until the Eagles lose their final football game.

That might rub some coaches the wrong way, especially those who need the limelight as much as they need oxygen. Wright welcomes the seasonal anonymity, content to work out his team's kinks in the deep recesses of the sports pages, thrilled that he can go to Phillies games, to his daughter's high school games, to a Bruce Springsteen concert, or just about anywhere else and draw only the slightest bit of attention.

"There's a lot of great things about coaching at Villanova, but one that I really enjoy is that during basketball season, you're like a pro team. You're big-time," Wright said. "But in the off-season, there's so many other sports teams and happenings you get to blend in. I go to a game and it's, 'Hey, Coach!' and that's it."

Wright, of course, is a slightly bigger deal now and he was, frankly, when he was initially hired, too. Villanova still was a national program when he was brought in but the program also needed a shot of adrenaline. He was the adrenaline.

Just as he did at Hofstra, he shamelessly stumped around campus drumming up interest. In campus cafeterias, he quite literally jumped on top of tables, asking the "Nova Nation" to come out and support the Wildcats. He even went so far as to reconfigure how his players took the court at the start of games; rather than running on the court directly from the locker room, he had the Wildcats come down the bleachers via an aisle in the middle of the student section.

Wright worked the recruiting trail even harder. In his first summer on the circuit, Wright landed what many considered the top class in the country. But the coup of bringing Randy Foye, Allan Ray, Curtis Sumpter, and Jason Fraser to Villanova stretched even beyond their talent; their geography was equally important. Ray, Sumpter, and Fraser were all from New York City powerhouse high schools, Foye from across the river in Newark. That they turned away from the beacon of St. John's and instead headed to Villanova signaled a significant shift in the college basketball, and the Big East, paradigm.

For Wright, it proved he could be a real player at the elite college basketball level.

But it also raised the stakes for the young coach.

"The thing about Villanova, it was always successful," Lange said. "Jay mentioned to me that everyone has won, and as soon as Jay steps on campus and gets that recruiting class, there are these huge expectations. I didn't think about it then but what was he? Thirty-nine? That's a big job."

And Wright had big dreams.

His goal was to create something more than a basketball team.

"He wanted to impart a culture," Lange said.

That culture began with Wright's favorite buzzword—attitude.

In the early years at Villanova, attitude was little more than a concept. Realizing he needed to foster it, Wright purposefully bolstered that early roster with a player he knew would understand it.

Baker Dunleavy was not a four-star recruit but he was the son of an NBA coach, the brother of an NBA player. He knew what it meant to win, knew what it took to be a good teammate.

"He knew he was bringing in this high-caliber class," Dunleavy said. "He needed someone to pass on his message to those players. That's where I came in."

Using Dunleavy to help guide his teammates, Wright imbued the idea of attitude, drill by drill, practice by practice, game by game. Sometimes he used sugar, often a little spice. Either way the message was delivered repeatedly. Staff members meted out points—for extra passes and smart plays—and slowly, the players realized that winning

Attitude Club meant more than just seeing your name on a special board in the locker room.

It meant you understood what Wright wanted. Even more, it meant you were following his lead.

"He's a prime example of always being hungry and humble," Jenkins said. "He's had a lot of success, but he's always looking to better himself and work harder."

Today ATTITUDE graces the walls at the Davis Center, Villanova's practice facility. Players wear blue bracelets emblazoned with the word around their wrists and Wright doles them out like candy at his summer camps to friends, colleagues, and fans.

When Villanova arrived in Houston for the Final Four in 2016, the managers went to the locker room to set up the space for what they hoped would be an extended weekend visit. They laid out the players' practice gear and divvied up who would sit where.

One of their first duties was to tape a piece of paper above the door.

It read, ATTITUDE.

Every time the Wildcats left for the court floor, they reached above their heads and slapped the word, a reminder of how they would approach that day.

So when they circled for that final huddle in the championship game, they carried attitude with them.

Father Rob, gifted with a non-coach's viewpoint, purposefully looked at each person in that moment. He, like everyone else seated around Wright, knew what the coach was going to call. He'd seen the Wildcats runs Nova hundreds of times in practice.

Rather than listen, he glanced around at the players and at Wright. He knows them all so well, and so much differently than anyone else on the Villanova bench. The players come to him for guidance and support. Some come for spiritual insight, others just to hear a different voice, one not tied directly to basketball.

Father Rob also has had his share of heart-to-hearts with Wright. He's watched him grow as a coach and as a person. He's seen firsthand how demanding Wright is, but also watched as he's tempered his own need for perfection with a willingness to allow his players the freedom to learn via mistakes.

What Father Rob saw in that moment, developed by a coach who learned from his dad that every player matters, who pushed his buddies to live outside of their comfort zones, who learned humility in college and risk-taking as an adult, was the culture Jay Wright wanted to create at Villanova.

"There was no fear in that huddle," Hagan said. "I knew whatever they were going to do, they were going to do it well. I didn't know if the ball would go in but it almost didn't matter."

As the horn sounded, warning the teams to return to the court, Wright called the Wildcats together for the final time. The players closed in around their coach, raised their hands together.

"Let's go, on three," Wright said.

"One, two three," they replied.

"Attitude."

Kris Jenkins stood out of bounds underneath the North Carolina basket, waiting to receive the ball from the official. Ryan Arcidiacono took his spot a few feet from Jenkins, just inside the free-throw line. Daniel Ochefu also slipped into the frontcourt, not far from Arcidiacono. Josh Hart and Phil Booth were positioned at the mid-court line, Hart hugging the sideline nearest to the team benches, Booth at the jump circle.

The play was designed so that Ochefu would set a screen for Arcidiacono at just about halfcourt. Hart would do the same for Booth, away from the ball. Jenkins would trail the dribbler. As the play unfolded, it was up to Arcidiacono to figure it all out, choosing one of the various options for Villanova's final shot of the game.

Of those five players, only one—Arcidiacono—was considered a top-50 recruit coming out of high school. None were high school All-Americans. In fact, the Villanova roster that would win the 2016 national championship boasted just one player named to a prestigious high school national team. And that player, Jalen Brunson, was the first McDonald's All-American to play for Jay Wright since 2010.

That's not entirely by chance.

"Villanova is built for a certain type of guy," Wright said.

The coach long ago identified who those guys were. They were athletes who valued winning over individual accomplishment, and even more, understood that the two can go hand in hand.

And then Wright lost sight of his own vision.

No one sees failure coming. It's sneaky, lying in wait, often hidden by the haze of happiness and success. It always feels sudden when it arrives, a surprise attack. In truth it usually builds slowly, leaving tell-tales in its wake. Except no one notices them, let alone cares to read them, until it's too late. What pass and feel like right and smart decisions in the moment don't reveal their true identities as grievous errors until the postmortem, after the failure is complete.

So it was for Villanova. Wright spent 11 years steadily and meticulously building his program, carefully choosing and then laying one block on top of the other. He landed a monster recruiting class in his first year, making a big splash when he lured Randy Foye, Allan Ray, Curtis Sumpter, and Jason Fraser to campus from their New York/New Jersey homes. Then he backed that group up with Mike Nardi and Will Sheridan, the first a feisty point guard from New Jersey, the second a blue-collar power forward from Delaware. A year later he brought in Kyle Lowry, a fearless and relentless guard out of Philadelphia. Along the way, the team found its identity as a haven for Mid-Atlantic ballplayers who weren't afraid to play tough.

It wasn't overnight success—it took three years for those players to coalesce into an NCAA Tournament team—and it wasn't all smooth sailing. The Wildcats endured some painful lessons and embarrassing mistakes. At the end of the 2002–03 season, the university suspended 12 basketball players for placing unauthorized long-distance phone calls using an employee's university phone access code (without the employee's knowledge). Though the Wildcats were able to stagger the suspensions in order to field a team, they were left with mostly walk-ons and practically no bench and finished the season with an embarrassing loss to Siena in the first round of the NIT.

The following year the NCAA placed Villanova on two years' probation, citing a series of minor violations that collectively added up to a big enough problem to put the program on notice.

The stains stung Wright especially hard. In a profession often labeled as overrun by renegades, rebels, and flat-out cheaters, his reputation took a hit, one that hurt especially because Wright long has held Villanova in such high esteem.

"He had to go on TV and do all of these interviews and explain everything," said former assistant coach Joe Jones, who is now head coach at Boston University. "He was unbelievable. I'm sitting there in my office at Villanova going, 'Oh my God. How's he doing this?' I knew it was crushing him, but he just owned it all."

Wright even felt the flames of the hot seat. Impatient fans, eyeing up the bevy of talented recruits Wright had amassed, figured they'd taste immediate success. Instead the Wildcats couldn't even win 20 games and spent Wright's first three seasons in the National Invitation Tournament, the NCAA Tournament's ugly stepbrother.

The pressure was never internal—"He was never on the hot seat with us," said Big East associate commissioner Vince Nicastro, who was Villanova's athletic director at the time—but it certainly existed in and around Philadelphia.

People accused the coach of being little more than an empty—albeit well-tailored—suit, some going so far as to suggest the coach be fired.

"There was definitely a lot of pressure from the outside," Wright said. "From our alumni, our fans, the media. I knew it."

But just as the cauldron might have lit, Wright and the Wildcats extinguished it. In the 2004–05 season, Villanova rolled to a 24–8 record and a tie for third place in the Big East Conference. Earning a No. 5 seed in the NCAA Tournament, the Wildcats beat New Mexico and Florida (they topped the Gators despite losing Sumpter, the team's second-leading scorer, to a torn ACL in the first half). Shorthanded without Sumpter, Villanova nonetheless pushed top-seeded North Carolina to the brink in the regional semifinal before losing 67–66.

A year later, the Wildcats won a then school-record 28 games, were ranked in the top 10 from the beginning of the season until the end, and earned the program's first No. 1 seed in the NCAA Tournament—all despite losing Sumpter to yet another torn ACL at the start of the year and using a four-guard lineup with the 6-foot-8 Sheridan as the lone big man.

The unorthodox style required the Wildcats to play out of their comfort zones. Shooters could no longer camp out on the arc and wait for others to do the rebounding. Everyone had to do the dirty work. But they loved it. The 6-foot-4 Foye nearly matched Sheridan in rebounding (5.8 to 6.3) and the 6-foot Lowry held his own, at 4.3.

Wright had constructed a team that included high-caliber players but ones with blue-collar work ethics, a combination that would become his teams' calling card, and a successful one. Ultimately Villanova would string together seven consecutive NCAA Tournament berths.

The high point came on March 28, 2009, in the TD Boston Garden.

Some of it ought to sound familiar.

NCAA Tournament regional final, Villanova and Pittsburgh are tied with 5.5 seconds left in the game. The Wildcats do not have a timeout to call. They don't need it. They know what to do. As soon as Pitt's Levance Fields ties the game with two made free throws, Reggie Redding goes under the basket as the inbounder. Scottie Reynolds takes his spot just inside the free-throw line, and Dante Cunningham hangs nearby. Shane Clark and Dwayne Anderson station themselves at midcourt, Anderson shaded toward the sideline, Clark near the jump circle.

Yes, the Wildcats are running Nova.

The read this time goes differently but it works as magically as it would seven years later. Redding lobs the ball to Cunningham, who one-touches a pass to a sprinting Reynolds. The savvy point guard dribbles ferociously straight down the lane and then goes up, floating a shot over the outstretched arms of Gilbert Brown. The ball slips through the basket and Villanova is in its first Final Four since its 1985 run to an unexpected championship.

"In that situation, you have four dribbles and a shot," Reynolds said after the game. "That's five seconds. All that goes in your head. That's why we practice that every day in practice so we can make an instinct play."

The Wildcats would go on to lose to North Carolina, the prohibitive favorite, in the national semifinals, but the loss didn't erase what Villanova accomplished. There are separators in college basketball, unseen lines that differentiate the value of one program over the next. Making the NCAA Tournament is one. Surviving the first weekend is another. Consistently doing the first, and then consistently doing the first and the second, creates an even smaller pool.

The ultimate divider, though, is the Final Four. To make it there marks a team as a bona fide, its coach as a success. Even the sport's one-hit wonders—George Mason in 2006, VCU in 2011, Wichita State in 2013—can get years of mileage and credibility from one appearance in the national semifinals.

For Villanova and Wright it meant even more, a sort of vindication for both. Despite the years of NCAA appearances leading up to 2009, Villanova was still classified among those one-hit wonders, living off of its 1985 national championship laurels. That 1985 team, a

No. 8 seed, remains the lowest-seeded team to win a national title and the Wildcats, who beat a Patrick Ewing–led Georgetown team that most assumed would walk away with the championship, quite literally played a near perfect game to do it. Villanova connected on 22 of its 28 field-goal attempts to win.

Though Villanova would go on to establish itself as a national program, that Cinderella image dies hard. And over time, as the college athletics landscape shifted dramatically, it would become even more difficult to shake. Today money talks, and no money talks more loudly than football money. Lucrative bowl games and even more lucrative television contracts have elevated football into college sports' largest cash cow. Villanova, though, does not have a top-level football program. The Wildcats compete at the Football Championship Subdivision level, one rung below the upper echelon. Its home stadium seats just 12,500, a far cry from the hundreds of thousands who pour into mammoth stadiums on fall Saturdays. The football-playing Wildcats are neither profiting off the rich coffers of the bowl system nor do they have a hefty television deal.

Plenty of people inside the business of college sports questioned if a school without such riches could compete at the highest level.

By stringing together year upon year of winning seasons, culminating with the Final Four in 2009, Villanova answered that with a resounding yes.

Meantime, Wright, the once popular young coach, silenced any detractors who thought his substance as a coach didn't meet his style.

Kentucky came calling that year, the bluest of the bluebloods expressing an interest in the Villanova coach after firing Billy Gillispie. Wright said no. The 76ers made overtures, too. Wright met with the bosses of the local NBA franchise who were looking to replace Tony

DiLeo. He said no to them as well, insisting that Villanova was where he wanted to be.

Wright's willingness to stay put only raised and legitimized the program's profile.

"Jay bought into what Villanova is and never saw that as a hindrance," said Father Rob Hagan, Villanova's associate director of athletics. "He used that culture to really enhance and promote what Villanova is and what he wants to do here."

But success creates a heady, intoxicating perfume and even the most level-headed are not immune to it. The Final Four capped an unbelievable run for the Wildcats—two Sweet 16 appearances, one Elite Eight, and one Final Four in five years—and suddenly a staff that often had to seek out amazing talent looked like the prettiest girl in school. Everyone was calling Villanova. Elite players wanted to come to campus. They liked Wright's style. They liked the way the Wildcats played. They wanted in.

Years later the decisions, both big and small, that led to the crash and burn were apparent. At the time no one saw anything but the chance to enjoy the fruits of their labor. The Wildcats had worked hard to establish a reputation and breed a culture, to create a brand that was both recognizable and successful. Finally they were reaping the rewards, sought after by players and respected by their peers.

"Villanova got so good so fast," said former Villanova assistant Billy Lange, who now is an assistant coach with the 76ers. "Things start to deteriorate underneath you and you don't even realize it's happening."

In hindsight, the first sign that things were deteriorating came a year later. The Wildcats finished 25–8 and were awarded a No. 2 seed in the NCAA Tournament, with an expectation of another deep run in March. Instead they were bounced early, upset in the second round by Saint Mary's. Villanova didn't play well in that game, but it's easy to rationalize and reconcile a March loss. Cinderella moments, after all, are what makes the NCAA Tournament so entertaining.

Besides, even as the Wildcats packed up their gear to leave Providence, they could look forward to the following season. Reynolds would graduate, but the Wildcats would dress five McDonald's All-Americans in 2010–11—Corey Stokes, Maalik Wayns, Taylor King, Dominic Cheek, and JayVaughn Pinkston—plus the New Jersey player of the year in Corey Fisher, and a consensus top-50 high school player in Isaiah Armwood.

The future was bright, so bright in fact that in August, ESPN announced it would be bringing its *College GameDay* set to campus.

But then came another crack. King, who had transferred into Villanova from Duke, left for USC. At the time the school announced King had voluntarily withdrawn from school. Years later King told CBSSports.com he was dismissed because he failed multiple drug tests.

Again, though, it was easy to push off any worries. King was a role player by the end of the previous season, and while losing him might hurt Villanova's depth, there was plenty of talent to go around.

And when the Wildcats started the 2010–11 season on an absolute tear, winning 16 of their first 17 games, both King and the loss to Saint Mary's were quickly forgotten.

Along with helping people forget the bad times, winning also can mask a team's warts. Even as his team was racking up victories, Wright sensed something wasn't quite right. He couldn't pin down the feeling, but it tickled the back of his mind. More than once he told Lange, who had left the staff to take over as head coach at Navy but remained a good friend, that things didn't feel right. It should have been the time of his life and the high point of his career, but he wasn't enjoying it.

To a man, every coach will say his favorite part of the job is his time on the court with his players—practice, games, those are the happiest places. But in an almost cruel fashion, the more a coach wins the more his off-the-court demands increase. Speaking engagements and donor events, media appearances and university functions, all conspire to tug a coach out of his office and away from his players.

That's where Wright, hot off the Final Four, found himself—in demand in all the wrong places.

"You get it going. You're so excited and so into it and you think it's never going to get old," Wright said. "And then you keep it going for a while and it does get old. All of the media, the alumni, the attention, you start thinking, *Oh man, we have to do this again?* You get tired and lazy, but you never think it's going to go away, so you don't worry. And then it goes away."

For Villanova it went away in a hurry, the season spinning out of control with a rapidity that was as unexpected as it was complete. From 16–1, the Wildcats' free fall began. It included an embarrassing loss to Rutgers, a lower-tier Big East team, and a humbling defeat at the hands of Pittsburgh in front of that *GameDay* audience. Villanova would win its last game of the season on February 19, 2011, the Wildcats eking out an overtime win against DePaul, which at the time had one Big East victory.

The bad win was merely a warmup for what was to come—a six-game, end-of-the-season slide into obscurity. Once ranked No. 6 in the country, the Wildcats lost to Syracuse, St. John's, Notre Dame, and Pittsburgh to finish the regular season; and to South Florida, the No. 15 seed, in the first round of the Big East Tournament. Now limping into the NCAA Tournament, the Wildcats slipped all the way to a No. 9 seed. When they were bounced in the first round by George Mason, few people were surprised.

In the span of two years, Villanova went from the hottest program in the country to the season's biggest disappointment.

"What happened to Villanova and Jay Wright?" one website pondered.

At that year's Final Four in Houston, Wright and Lange met for lunch in a hotel lobby restaurant, two old friends reconnecting to talk about their careers.

The son of a basketball coach, Lange began his own collegiate coaching career at Philadelphia University, serving as an assistant to Basketball Hall of Famer Herb Magee. By 1999, Lange, only 27 years old, had his own head coaching spot, leading the U.S. Merchant Marine Academy to two league titles in three years. Wright was down the road at Hofstra at the time and the two struck up a friendship. When Wright got the job at Villanova, he quickly named Lange his director of basketball operations.

Lange spent three years on Wright's staff, helping to establish the program's identity and culture.

By the time they met in Houston in 2011, Lange was in his seventh year as a head coach at Navy, working steadily to turn the service academy into a competitive program. There was no grand plan, no design to bring Lange back to Villanova. But a month later, when assistant coach Chris Walker left Wright's staff to go to Texas Tech, Wright immediately called Lange.

That niggling feeling that something wasn't right, that his time was being drained, still bugged Wright. In Lange, he saw a potential solution.

"I think he felt like he could use someone that, if he had to take off for three days and do some university event, he'd have someone he trusted to run the show," Lange said. "I knew the core values of the program and I could fill in."

Rare is the coach who would voluntarily leave a Division I head coaching job for an assistant's position. But for Lange, the reality of coaching at Navy—where the rigors of campus life and the military commitment after make for a difficult sell—and the draw of Villanova, maybe even the chance to one day succeed Wright, were impossible to turn down.

Lange remembered what Wright had told him, that things didn't feel right, but he figured it was merely the outside demands that were weighing on the coach. Lange looked at the returning roster and figured he'd slide right back into the successful program he'd left in 2004.

He quickly figured out how wrong he was.

The Wildcats finished 13–19 in 2011–12, the worst finish in Wright's tenure at Villanova, the most losses by a Villanova team in program history.

During that season, Villanova lost to Saint Louis and Santa Clara. Rival Saint Joseph's beat the Wildcats by 16 and South Florida topped them by 17. From the beginning of January until the end of February, Villanova won just four times. The Wildcats ended the season losing six of their final eight games, including a humbling 56–47 loss to South Florida in the second round of the Big East Tournament.

As bad as it looked from the outside, it was even worse internally.

"Everybody was just out for themselves," JayVaughn Pinkston would later say of that season.

Looking back, Wright knows he should have seen it coming, that his lost joy should have been a sign of a deeper problem but he, like everyone else, was blindsided.

"I remember once, he said to me, 'It's so hard not to get intoxicated with fame,'" Lange said.

Lange didn't understand entirely what Wright meant at the time but it all made perfect sense later, after it all went bad.

When he arrived at the intersection of the old ways that made him successful and the riches from all of that success, Wright unwittingly chose a different path. The same man who spent so much time cultivating an attitude and a culture at Villanova, who believed in the core values his father once used as a coach, had abandoned his own approach.

He started to value skill over character. He got caught up in recruiting wars, worrying more about beating out other schools for top-level players rather than identifying which players he really ought to take.

As soon as he returned to Villanova, Lange saw the changes. He told Wright as much, reminding him the message he was selling to players now wasn't the same one he was using when he was first hired. The players weren't the same, either. But Lange also understood how it happened, how Wright—distracted, spread too thin, and slightly starry eyed—didn't put the same time and thought into decisions as he once did.

"Every coach in the Big East would have taken those players," Lange said. "It's not that they weren't talented or heralded. They were. But they weren't coming to Villanova for the same reason Coach wanted them to come. For a lot of coaches, that doesn't matter. For Jay at Villanova, it's his dream job. It matters."

Wright's mistakes weren't unique.

With so much attention to recruiting—websites rank and re-rank players as early as middle school—coaches and their programs are judged as much by the quality of the class they land as the number of games that they win. Never mind that the true merit of a recruiting class can't be properly evaluated until it has produced—or failed to produce—at the end of its collegiate career. Signing a top recruiting class is big news, and done well can even perpetuate itself, creating a pipeline for the future. Talented players want to be associated with the schools and coaches that attract the best talent, and so one top class often begets another.

But sometimes the carousel spins so fast it is difficult to get off.

"It becomes uncontrollable," Wright said.

The challenges in recruiting, and then coaching, elite players are everywhere. Ranking athletes naturally breeds an expectation, whereby top high school players are expected to translate seamlessly into top college players. Little, if any, regard is given to elevated competition at the collegiate level or a lack of experience. Elite prospects are judged immediately and relentlessly as college freshmen and anything less than a string of stellar results can lead to the dreaded "overrated" tag.

"It's expectations versus reality for kids," said Villanova associate head coach Baker Dunleavy. "They deserve time to adjust. They deserve time to become college basketball players but because of the outside expectations, or their rankings were so high, they're expected to hit the ground running."

And when they don't the real trouble starts for everyone.

With so much concentration today on professional basketball, being a good college basketball player has been completely devalued. Plenty of college athletes have dealt with feelings of failure because they did not play in the NBA, even if they've had successful and lucrative careers overseas.

Worse, kids who come to college expecting to be in the pro ranks within a year and aren't good enough to turn pro immediately despair.

"We had some guys who were juniors and seniors and not happy about it," Wright said. "They thought they'd be out early."

That need and almost desperation to move on and move out quickly, to realize an expectation made by a website ranking, coupled with the NBA age limit that requires a player to compete at least one year in college, has turned the college game into little more than a protracted NBA audition.

Everything—playing time, points scored, shots taken—is viewed through the prism of a future pro career rather than the impact on the college team.

"Nobody," Ochefu said, "cares about winning a championship as a senior anymore. They just want to get to the league. And that's a shame."

A coach, then, has to walk an almost impossible tightrope. He has to appease his player's individual needs yet also achieve the greater good of team success. Coaches aren't fired if they don't get players to the NBA. They're fired because they don't win enough games.

A select few teams—Kentucky in 2012 and Duke in 2015—have managed to do both but those teams are rarities.

Villanova never was, never intended to be, nor likely ever will be one of those teams.

"They can have all freshmen and sophomores and compete on a national level," Dunleavy said. "We're not that way. We're at our best when we have juniors and seniors."

Following that nadir of a 2011–12 season, two players—Dominic Cheek and Maalik Wayns—would declare for the draft and leave Villanova early. Two more transferred out—Markus Kennedy, a Philadelphia native, went to Southern Methodist in Dallas; point guard Ty Johnson headed to South Carolina. And Wright would do some serious introspection. Lange recalls more than a few long car rides down Interstate 95 when the two, on the road recruiting, would talk about what went wrong and how to fix it.

Wright was fortunate. At some schools a 13–19 finish would merit a strict talking to from an athletic director, even a university president or chancellor, and put a coach on notice to produce or else. The

Villanova administration never pressured Wright or threatened to fire him.

"Sure, there was pressure from the rank and file fan base, which I get because they're so passionate and enthusiastic about our program," Nicastro said. "But from our leadership, our president, the board, impactful donors, everyone had a great deal of confidence in Jay."

Instead of worrying about his job security, Wright was afforded the luxury of worrying about doing his job better. Having Lange and Dunleavy on staff helped. Both were there when Wright got things started at Villanova, Lange as an assistant, Dunleavy as a player. They could and did remind him of the difference between what Villanova had been and what it had become.

The error was simple—Wright took guys instead of Villanova guys.

"The first time, it was baptism by fire," Dunleavy said. "In a different way, this was just as difficult. You're humbled, obviously. But there are only two ways to go about it. You try to find a way to get a quick fix or you go to work and dig deep. I think we all saw that example from Coach."

One of the least newsworthy yet most critical decisions Wright made was to turn Jason Donnelly, his onetime bench coach, into the assistant to the head coach. Paramount among Donnelly's duties is working with alumni groups and at fund-raisers, and serving as a liaison between the university and former players—namely all of the ancillary assignments that occupied so much of Wright's time and removed him from his real job of coaching.

The bigger, more difficult task, was reconstructing his lineup. At least Wright was clear in what he wanted to do.

"The goal is to make decisions that are difficult and may get people upset with you, in recruiting, in the media, and with alumni, but to stick to your core values," Wright said. "And those are the only things that matter—your players, your coaches, and your family."

Wright already had identified the first pieces to his reconstructed foundation, three older and wiser players who would help give the program the stability it had been missing.

Mouphtaou Yarou, who emigrated in 2007 from Benin to the United States, was a rising senior who steadily improved yearly. After missing some of his freshman season with hepatitis B, Yarou had grown from a sometimes contributor, averaging 4.5 points per game, to a full-time starter contributing 11.3 points and 8.2 rebounds in his junior season.

In James "Tahj" Bell, Wright had a rising junior who had willingly and patiently bided his time. After playing just nine minutes per game as a freshman, Bell averaged 23 minutes in his sophomore season.

Wright also would add Tony Chennault to his roster. A talented player out of Philadelphia who was once a McDonald's All-America nominee, Chennault had played two seasons at Wake Forest but transferred closer to home when his mother fell ill. Wright liked Chennault's game. He loved his maturity and leadership.

The coach also intended to rely heavily on two soon-to-be sophomores, hoping their experience on a losing Villanova team would fuel them to correct things in the future.

Darrun Hilliard played sparingly as a freshman, averaging 4.8 points per game, but he was exactly the sort of player Wright loved. Raised in the gritty steel town of Bethlehem, Pennsylvania, Hilliard never had been handed anything. He scored more than 1,400 points in his high school career but fell below the recruiting radar, labeled just a three-star recruit.

His start at Villanova was difficult. Pressed into service as a point guard after Ty Johnson was injured, he averaged seven points per game early but then scored 42 in the last 15 games of the season combined. Young for his grade—he enrolled at just 17—Hilliard doubted himself and his skills, even contemplated transferring.

That Hilliard stuck it out told Wright all he needed to know about his player's character.

"He trusts everybody here, so when everybody told him, 'You're good, man, you're going to be good here,' he believed it and continued to work," Wright told CSNPhilly.

JayVaughn Pinkston's path was altogether different, and decidedly more complicated. Pinkston graduated from Bishop Loughlin High School in Brooklyn as a McDonald's All-American. On the basketball hype spectrum, there is no more dangerous pairing than being a New York kid with big credentials. Everyone assumed Pinkston would make the requisite college one year fly-by and move on to the NBA.

Instead he spent what he thought would be his first and only year in college stacking boxes at a warehouse near the Villanova campus, trying to stretch a paycheck to cover his one-bedroom apartment. In November 2010, in what would have been his freshman year, Pinkston was arrested and later charged with assault stemming from a fight at an off-campus apartment. The university immediately barred him from basketball and, following a disciplinary review, suspended him from school for the spring semester. He finished up one semester's worth of coursework but never played for the Wildcats. As part of his punishment, he also was barred from campus, which meant he could not work out with his teammates or even watch their games.

Rather than allow him to come home and fall victim to the tough neighborhood, Pinkston's mother, Kerry, insisted he stay nearer to campus and work. While his teammates traveled the country to play basketball, Pinkston stacked boxes.

"I realized I did this to myself," Pinkston would say later of the punishment. "So I had to deal with it."

His reward for sticking it out, rather than transferring or quitting? A freshman year where the team simply could not win.

That frustrating finish and Pinkston's credentials as a former high school All-American with ties to the rich New York basketball scene made Pinkston perhaps the most crucial piece in determining Villanova's immediate future. The coaches desperately needed him to be on board, to believe in the message the staff was sending, and to make sure his teammates bought in, too.

Consequently, Wright had more than a few heart-to-hearts with Pinkston. What he learned, though, was that Pinkston didn't really need to be sold. Pinkston is fiercely loyal and felt beholden to a coach who stuck by him through his suspension. While others around him thought he should have eyed an immediate run to the NBA, Pinkston never saw himself as a one-and-done player. He put a premium on teamwork and wanted to right Villanova's ship.

"His reputation was key, whether he was down with Villanova and the coaches or not," Lange said. "All of the guys were sort of looking at how JayVaughn reacted and when he said he was down with Villanova, that was big. I don't know what would have happened if he didn't see it that way."

The only two players more critical to Villanova's turnaround than Pinkston, interestingly enough, were the two who had never put on a Villanova uniform. While the program was devolving into that 13–19 season, Daniel Ochefu and Ryan Arcidiacono were finishing up their final year of high school. A year earlier, they'd each pledged their allegiance to the Wildcats but had committed to a program that was in the midst of a glorious run, not one losing game after game.

Ochefu, who was boarding at the Westtown School just 17 miles from the Villanova campus, remembers sneaking away from study halls to watch televised Wildcats games in the dormitory lounges. Later he'd head back to his room and his friends would wonder what had made him so angry.

"What was I thinking? I was thinking about changing schools," Ochefu said. "I heard so much stuff. Things like, 'Oh, you guys are going to suck next year.' I was wondering if I should switch."

Ochefu's inner circle—his parents and high school coach—wouldn't let him and instead reminded him why he liked the school so much in the first place. Admittedly skeptical, Ochefu opted to honor his decision.

Meantime, up the road in Langhorne, Pennsylvania, Arcidiacono was recuperating from serious back surgery. Unable to play he had nothing but time on his hands—time to watch the Villanova season go down the tubes. Unlike Ochefu, though, Arcidiacono never wavered. His parents are both Villanova graduates and his affinity for the place runs deep. He spent more than a few nights alongside his father, Joe, watching games and wondering what in the world was going on with the Wildcats, but not once considered switching schools.

"Honestly I looked at it as an opportunity to help the team out," Arcidiacono said. "I wasn't going to come in and try to score a million points. It was, what do they need me to do?"

That was exactly the attitude—or Attitude—Wright was looking for. Both players were highly sought after—Ochefu would also seriously consider Georgetown, while Arcidiacono turned down Florida in favor of Villanova—and certainly they had designs on, and would eventually realize, professional careers. But first they wanted to come to Villanova, to invest in and be part of Villanova.

They embodied the culture that Wright was trying to reestablish. He is not averse to recruiting players who want to leave for college early, or against coaching elite players. He just wants people who, no matter how short their tenure at Villanova, how high their ranking, make Villanova a priority and feel a connection to the school.

"It's not about me personally; it's what fits Villanova," Wright said. "Every guy we had, all the way back to Kyle and Randy, they came to be a part of Villanova. And if that got them to be a first-round pick after their sophomore year like Kyle, great. If it got them to be a four-year, college-degree NBA player like Randy, great. If four years got them to the Elite Eight and a career as a rapper like Will Sheridan, great. But they wanted to be a part of this place. That's what we've found that we wanted."

Ochefu and Arcidiacono arrived at Villanova in the summer before their freshman season. They took summer school classes and readied for preseason conditioning and individual workouts. They knew the jump to college would be tough. They underestimated just how tough.

Intent on rebuilding attitude and culture as much as developing fitness, Wright relentlessly worked his players. He may have understood that he made mistakes, but he didn't like it and he damned sure was going to make sure it didn't happen again.

Arcidiacono says now it was the hardest summer of his life. Ochefu recalled that, after his first workout in the weight room, the assistant coaches came up to him to make sure he was okay.

One day the Wildcats spent 45 minutes working on nothing but defensive slides, chasing after a towel wrapped up into a ball. The next they'd just run—sprints and suicides and laps.

"I think Coach was trying to weed out who wasn't going to stick with the culture, who didn't get it," Ochefu said.

In the movie version, the Wildcats figure it out immediately and sail on to great things. In reality Villanova opened the 2012–13 season 3–3, including an 18-point loss at home to Ivy League member Columbia.

Joe Arcidiacono remembers taking his son out for pizza after that game, hoping to cheer him up. Instead, Ryan sat morosely, mulling over the game.

"I stink. We stink. This is awful," Arcidiacono said over and over again.

By the start of January, things looked better. On January 2, the Wildcats won their sixth game in a row, beating St. John's in overtime. The game served as something of a coming-out party for Arcidiacono. In his first Big East Conference game, the freshman scored 32 points. The players, understandably, were feeling pretty good about themselves.

The coach was not. To be frank, St. John's was an average team, just 8–4 before the game, and the Wildcats did not play well. They committed six turnovers in the game's first eight minutes. Wright knew his team's record was something of a façade, and by then he'd had just about enough of results masking deficiencies and weaknesses. Having been fooled once by winning, Wright wasn't about to make the same mistake again.

After the win, Villanova did not have another game on the schedule for a full week. School was out for the holidays. Practice was on for the Wildcats. Each morning they'd slog through the snow and trudge across campus to the gym, leaving the dorms as early as 6:00 AM. They'd practice for hours and repeat the process in the afternoon. At the end of each night, they were too tired to even speak, much less hang out, with one another.

"I remember guys saying if they slipped on ice they'd be cool with it because it would get them out of practice," Ochefu said.

The boot camp wasn't a magic elixir. These Wildcats, young in age and new to Wright's expectations, were never going to be consistent, and so the rest of the season continued on erratically. Villanova would go on to lose five of its next eight games but then show signs that maybe Wright's seeds were taking root. In consecutive games, the Cats upset No. 5 Louisville and No. 3 Syracuse, becoming the first unranked team to beat two top-five opponents in a season in three years. They'd defeat No. 17 Marquette and No. 5 Georgetown, but also would lose to a sub-.500 Seton Hall team and a struggling Providence squad.

They'd finish a more than respectable 20–14 and earn a ticket back to the NCAA Tournament. But the biggest measure of where the program stood wasn't in the win-loss column; it was with what Wright and the Wildcats had learned.

"You don't think it's going to happen, that you're going to get great. It happens," Wright said. "You don't think it's going to get old. It gets old. You don't think it's going to go away. It goes away. Then you know enough to wonder, is it going to come back? Can we get it back?"

The following season, Villanova would offer a more definitive answer. Hot off a 4–0 start, Villanova traveled to the Bahamas for the Battle for Atlantis, one of a collection of destination tournaments that dot the college basketball schedule around Thanksgiving and Christmas. The unranked Wildcats easily dispatched of Southern California 94–79 in the opening round of the tournament, setting up a meeting with No. 2 Kansas.

Late in the game, Villanova would give back all of a 57–46 lead and trailed by one with under 30 seconds to play. After forcing a jump ball with 12.4 seconds remaining, the Wildcats inbounded the ball from beneath their own basket. Arcidiacono cut from the low blocks on the right side of the net, and using a screen from Josh Hart, popped out on the opposite wing, directly in front of his own bench. At that point, the freshman had missed each of the five shots he'd taken, all three-pointers.

Fed the ball by Hiliard, he calmly drained the game-winning three, securing the upset of the Jayhawks.

The next night Villanova, trailing by 12 points with 11 minutes left in the game, rallied to force overtime and ultimately upset No. 23 Iowa to win the Battle for Atlantis title.

That night, Arcidiacono, Ochefu, and their two walk-on class-mates, Pat Farrell and Henry Lowe, got together. They reminisced about their brutal freshmen season, the price they paid for that 13–19 finish. They talked about winning the Battle for Atlantis, and then they considered what they were seeing in their team and in their teammates. Pinkston and Hilliard, the lone leftovers from the 13–19 team, told them how bad it had been. The disconnected locker room, the individuals who never quite came together to make a whole.

The players realized, without even being told, that in those three games in the Bahamas, the change was really beginning.

"A winning culture," Ochefu called it, "where winning was important but the culture was even more important."

No one can remember who said it—maybe Farrell or Lowe.

But someone came up with a nickname for the Villanova Class of 2016.

The Redemption Class.

The North Carolina players—Marcus Paige, Brice Johnson, Isaiah Hicks, and Justin Jackson—huddled together on the floor, Paige motioning behind him toward the basket the Tar Heels would have to defend. He said something to his teammates and they nodded their heads in agreement.

UNC assistant coach C.B. McGrath walked up the stairs from the bench and onto the elevated court, shouting some last-minute instructions to his players. Jay Wright, at first heading away from the action, turned abruptly to say something to his players.

Everyone was plotting and planning for the final 4.7 seconds of the national championship game. Everyone, that is, except Daniel Ochefu who, in the midst of the tensest moment of the college basketball season, chose to mop the floor.

The Villanova senior walked over to the young boy assigned the task of cleaning up the wet spots on the court and politely took the mop out of his hand to do the job himself. He pushed the mop back and forth a few times, stretching it to reach a spot official John Higgins pointed to.

Everyone got a good chuckle out of Ochefu. The boy charged with the clean-up job smiled, and the NCAA folks seated at the nearby press table all grinned as well. On the CBS telecast, a bemused Bill Raftery joked, "I could use him around my house."

Only Ochefu wasn't playing around. On the previous play, as he tried in vain to prevent Marcus Paige's game-tying, double-pump three-pointer, Ochefu had skidded across the floor in that very spot, leaving a streak of sweat in his wake. That small piece of slippery real estate, he knew, could prove to be the difference between a Villanova national title and overtime.

Two years earlier, when Ochefu and his classmates dubbed themselves Villanova's Redemption Class, they decided the nickname would be about more than simply redeeming a program from a losing season. It would be about redeeming, and redefining, what it meant to be a Villanova basketball player.

"You play hard. You play smart," Ochefu said. "You work together as a unit. You do the little things."

That's exactly who Ochefu had become by his senior year. Rarely the leading scorer in a game, hardly ever the first option on offense, he had become a critical part of Villanova's success by doing a million little things. In film study, it was Ochefu who asked the most questions and soaked in the most information. In a team huddle, it was Ochefu who would correct a teammate's mistake, sometimes even before his head coach could. Blessed with a high IQ and an ebullient personality, he gave thoughtful answers to reporters' questions but didn't sugarcoat his opinions.

And so in that moment when everyone else was thinking about the big picture, Ochefu keyed on the small one and mopped.

Asked to imagine his younger self, a self-described smart-mouthed rebel, with the mop in his hand, Ochefu laughed.

"Uh, no," Ochefu laughed. "You could say I've always had some trouble with authority."

How did a would-be rabble-rouser turn into a first-team cleaner-upper? Maybe the best place to search for the explanation is in Nigeria. That's where Ochefu's father, Hassan, was born and raised. His father,

Ochefu's grandfather, was a military governor there and the family, with a tree dotted with doctors and lawyers and academicians, was widely respected.

But Ochefu didn't know any of that, didn't even know most of his extended family. He was born in the United States. Hassan emigrated here in the 1980s, met and married his wife, Elizabeth, who is from Cameroon, and settled in Maryland. The couple had four kids—Daniel, Marie, Anthony, and Ashley—and were contentedly raising them as typical American kids. Daniel, the oldest, immediately gravitated to the basketball courts. Hassan is 6-foot-6, an uncle stands 6-foot-8, and Ochefu, clearly gifted with the paternal genes, quickly became a force among the peewees on the court. The 12-year-old was finishing up the summer AAU circuit, wrapping up a national showcase, when his parents dropped a bit of news on him.

After lengthy discussion and some pushback from Elizabeth, they'd decided to move to Nigeria.

"We wanted the children to know their family back home, to get a sense of belonging and know where they are coming from," said Elizabeth, who admitted she was initially less than keen about moving away from her friends in the States. "Society here offers so much to kids, we wanted to teach them not to take it for granted. We wanted them to go back, to see what it was like for other people, what it was to not have everything at your fingertips."

Knowing that Ochefu, as their oldest child, would struggle the most with the move, Hassan and Elizabeth agreed to let him come to it gradually. They left in the fall and he stayed behind, living in Maryland with Elizabeth's sister. Over the Christmas break, Hassan flew back to get Ochefu, ostensibly to fly him to Nigeria for a "vacation." But he and Elizabeth also knew that Ochefu was missing his parents and siblings terribly. They rightly banked that his need for his family would help him overcome his reluctance to move to Nigeria.

They were right. Ochefu stayed in Nigeria after the vacation ended. That's not to say the reunion with the family made the transition any easier for Ochefu. He missed his friends. He missed his school. He missed just being an American pre-teen. And he really missed basketball.

"I was just thrown to the wolves," he said. "Just had to go and figure it out."

Normal everyday things that Ochefu took for granted weren't guaranteed. With power outages rampant, the family relied frequently on a generator, and daily running water wasn't always a certainty.

For Ochefu, though, the everyday struggles were nothing compared to understanding his place in the societal hierarchy. Children speak when they are spoken to, not when they feel like voicing an opinion, and deference to one's elders is the backbone of the Nigerian culture. But by elders, Nigerians mean *anyone* older. A child is not only expected to be respectful to an adult but to an older child as well.

That, needless to say, did not go over well with the boy who routinely had a problem with authority. It's not that Ochefu was a bad kid—he just didn't like being told what to do. If someone said he had to be somewhere at 7:00 PM, he'd intentionally arrive at 7:15. Why? Mostly because he could.

And now here he was in Nigeria, expected not only to cede that control to grownups, but to older kids, as well.

"I had a big problem with that," Ochefu said. "I was like, 'Why is this sixth grader telling me, some fifth grader, what to do? And why do I have to listen?'"

It didn't help that Ochefu was so much bigger than the other kids in his grade. He felt older than them and they, sensing his size gave him an air of superiority, were even more distrustful of him. At first, he spent a great deal of time on his own or playing basketball in an adult men's league, but slowly, with the help of his older cousins—the "cool" kids in school—he better navigated the social stratospheres.

Academics were another story. Every morning Ochefu boarded a bus at 5:00 AM to begin the four-hour trek to school. The school building wasn't that far but the chaotic, clogged traffic in the country extended the trip. Once he arrived, he'd encounter a curriculum more rigorous than any he experienced back in the U.S. He skipped sixth grade, a move he still isn't sure was a great idea, and was faced with a demanding academic schedule that he said included coursework he wouldn't face in the United States until the 10th grade.

And to make matters worse, Nigerian teachers still practiced corporal punishment. Any excuse the authority-challenging Ochefu tried to come up with fell on deaf ears and resulted in a good whack.

"It was a definite eye-opener for Daniel," Elizabeth said. "But he learned that being grumpy isn't going to get you anywhere. There are a whole bunch of people around you who have it much harder, so there's no point in being grumpy."

Over time Ochefu mixed in well. He made friends and found his footing. He even reluctantly put down his basketball and started kicking a soccer ball. He found he was pretty good at it, too. His height gave the midfielder a decided advantage and Ochefu thinks, had he not eventually moved back to the U.S., he could have been a professional soccer player.

But the tug of the hardcourt was hard to resist. Even as he was working on his soccer game, Ochefu would find time at least once a month to play basketball. More often than not he was alone—there simply weren't many other kids interested in the game—but he still played faithfully.

Two years into the relocation, Hassan and Elizabeth realized that, though their son was making the best of the situation, his heart was elsewhere. "Basketball, it was a love we couldn't suppress," Elizabeth said. "He festered." They believed the move had made the desired impression on their son. It grounded him, they thought, and gave him the appreciation for his own life they'd been seeking. Finally they agreed that, armed with his newfound maturity, it was only fair to allow Ochefu to pursue his own dream.

When Ochefu was 13, his parents sent him to a 76ers overnight camp in the Pocono Mountains, in northeastern Pennsylvania. He quickly caught the eye of one of the counselors. Years and a lifetime earlier, Seth Berger made a career for himself as the founder of And1, a basketball shoe and gear company that featured street ballers in various mixtape competitions. The graduate of the University of Pennsylvania's prestigious Wharton business school cashed out after the company's profits peaked and, with a young family to raise, looked for a simpler lifestyle. The former high school point guard turned to coaching, landing a spot as an assistant coach at the Westtown School, a private Quaker school just outside of Pennsylvania.

By the time he went to work that 76ers camp, Berger was the school's head coach.

A series of plays sold him on Ochefu.

"He ran the ball three successive times as a 13-year-old big and the youngest guy on the court, playing with 14- and 15-year-olds," Berger said. "And he ran back after missing a layup as opposed to being disappointed and hanging his head. As a 13-year-old, he got it."

Berger approached the Ochefu family about letting their son come to Westtown. They decided to wait one more year, until Ochefu was headed into his freshman season, but knew immediately the setup would be perfect. Though Ochefu was ready to move back to the U.S., his family wasn't. They planned to stay in Nigeria—and would for Ochefu's first three years of high school.

But Westtown offers boarding accommodations for its students, which meant Ochefu would have a place to live, and Berger agreed to let him stay with his family in the summer and during school breaks. Equally important, the school's Quaker principles and strict disciplinary rules appealed to the deeply religious Elizabeth.

The transition went remarkably well. Though Ochefu missed his family, he was mature enough to handle the separation and his eagerness to play basketball kept him going. He went to work with Berger almost immediately. Ochefu already was a deft passer and solid ball-handler for his size, so Berger focused on improving Ochefu's shot, teaching him how to score facing the basket. On more than one occasion, Berger ran into Ochefu's hardheadedness, but over time Berger also learned how to handle it. The stubbornness, the coach realized, was borne out of Ochefu's intelligence. It wasn't enough that he be told to do something; Ochefu needed to be told why he should do it.

Berger remembers one game, a big one against Our Savior New American, a team that featured future St. John player Chris Obekpa. The coach kept chiding Ochefu for being a little too quick with his shot from the low post. No matter what Berger said, Ochefu rushed, missing easy opportunities and failing to get fouled as he might have if he collected himself first. Finally player and coach struck a deal—every time Ochefu caught the ball, he'd have to count, "One Nigeria" in his head before shooting. If he didn't keep his promise—and since Berger would be counting on the sideline as well, he would know—Ochefu would be out of the game.

"He gets the ball and he puts it up as fast as he can," Berger said. "He comes down the floor waving his finger at me because it went in. I said, 'Uh uh. You come right here.' I pulled him out of the game and he was fuming but with Daniel, he's so smart, you can't trick him. You have to show him."

Once Berger and Ochefu found a common ground, Ochefu blossomed. He spent hours in the gym before and after practice, and even in the off-season, constantly trying to hone his skills. By the end of his first year of high school, Ochefu already had received his first recruiting letter—a missive from Notre Dame.

As Ochefu continued to improve his team proved the immediate beneficiary, reaching the Friends School League playoffs in his sophomore year, the league finals in his junior year, and amassing a 52–25 record in three seasons. He averaged 16 points and 12 rebounds as a junior, earned *Sports Illustrated* player of the week honors, and climbed into the top 100 national rankings for his class. No surprise, then, that college coaches quickly came calling.

Georgetown, Temple, Texas, and Villanova all expressed interest in Ochefu.

The Maryland native was particularly enamored of Georgetown. Though his family had since returned from Nigeria and settled in nearby Exton, Pennsylvania, the ties to the D.C. area remained strong, as did the Hoyas' allure.

As for Villanova, though the program was coming off its 2009 Final Four run, some questioned whether it was the right fit for a big man with Ochefu's skills. Today, spurred on by the success of the

Golden State Warriors, small ball is all the rage. Eyeing the quick-footed and sharpshooting skills of players such as Stephen Curry and Klay Thompson, other teams—both professional and collegiate—have tried to mimic their offenses, putting a premium on guard play.

Villanova had gone to small ball years ahead of the trend. After forward Curtis Sumpter tore his ACL during the 2005 NCAA Tournament, Wright had no choice but to use a four-guard lineup for the Wildcats' regional-semifinal game against North Carolina. Then, when Sumpter tore his other ACL at the start of the 2006 season, the coach was forced again to go with the unorthodox lineup for the entirety of the season. It worked to the tune of an Elite Eight run. Soon people forgot that Wright went small out of necessity and the school earned a reputation as "Guard U." It's not that the Wildcats didn't produce talented big men—Dante Cunningham was a second-round NBA pick—but most, including Cunningham, were more athletic forwards than prototypical centers.

At 6-foot-11, Ochefu was a traditional post player and some thought he'd be better served at a school that put more of a premium on his position. Wright wouldn't hear of such criticism.

"I'll give you a little recruiting pitch right here," Wright said. "You want to come and play with these great guards. If you're with great guards, they're going to get you the ball and the other team is not going to double-team you and you're going to be able to score."

When it came to convincing Ochefu to come to Villanova, though, it wasn't Wright who threw the winning pitch. It was Father Rob Hagan, the school's associate athletic director and team chaplain. Villanova is a Catholic university, founded by the Order of Saint Augustine, and though not everyone who attends the school is Roman Catholic, the school does not hide its religious ties.

Nor does Wright, a Catholic himself. He doesn't force religion on anyone but there is a spiritual component to the program. Hagan attends every Villanova game home and away, taking his place on the far end of the Wildcats bench. Before tipoff and after the buzzer sounds, he gathers the team together for a prayer and a brief talk, and encourages and welcomes players and staff to his office if they want to talk.

For some recruits, those religious ties have no bearing. But with Ochefu, the Villanova coaching staff did its homework. They knew how much the role of faith could factor in his decision.

"Daniel's mom wanted him to be an Augustinian," Hagan said.

He was only half kidding. Elizabeth admits she would have loved it if her son became a priest. She knew that wasn't likely to happen but, absent of a future in the seminary, she at least wanted Ochefu to attend a college deeply rooted in the family's Catholic faith.

"There's a period in your life, you go to college and you sort of forget everything you've been taught, especially with religion," Elizabeth said. "I thought at least if he's close to home, I can take him to Mass, and make sure he goes to confession."

Other Catholic schools, Elizabeth said, downplayed their association with the Church, but knowing how much Elizabeth valued her son's religious education, Villanova included a visit with Hagan on Ochefu's schedule. The family sat together in the theater room just outside of the basketball office reception area.

"I just kind of sat there with my dad," Ochefu said. "She did all of the talking."

Elizabeth didn't make the final decision, naturally, but her opinion carried a great deal of weight. Ochefu sat down and made a checklist, itemizing the things he wanted in his college basketball experience. Though he still thought he was leaning toward Georgetown, when he filled out the list—which included everything from his comfort with the coaching staff to the school's social scene—he found more marks next to Villanova than any other school on his list.

In May 2011, excited to close the door on the exhausting recruiting process before his senior year began, Ochefu verbally committed to Villanova. Six months later he made the commitment official, signing his binding letter of intent with the Wildcats.

But that commitment would be tested in May 2012 when Ochefu withdrew from Westtown. It was his decision to leave—he transferred to nearby Downingtown East High School and a month later would receive his diploma there—but it came only after Ochefu was involved in a disciplinary issue at Westtown. The incident, all parties agree, was minor. Villanova never balked at admitting Ochefu and the Westtown School not only has since welcomed him back to campus to celebrate his national championship, his younger brother, Anthony, is playing basketball there.

The best way to classify it? Ochefu's admitted stubborn refusal to cede to authority running headlong into a school with strict rules.

"It was minor, very minor, and actually, having gone through it in high school, I think it saved Daniel from going through it in college," Berger said. "He took responsibility. He didn't blame anybody else. He basically said, 'I screwed up.'"

That trouble with authority didn't stop magically when Ochefu got to college, however. He was never disrespectful but he took his time warming up to Wright. He wanted the same thing he got from Berger—explanations and reasoning. Wright, coming off that 13–19 season, didn't exactly have the time to give a freshman the rationale behind his every decision.

Berger remembers more than a few phone calls, text messages, and meetings, Ochefu trying to get from his high school coach what his college coach wouldn't supply—answers. Berger explained that as a college coach, Wright's first charge was to win basketball games, not to give detailed explanations to his new big man. The two butted heads for quite some time.

"My freshman year wasn't a smooth ride at all," Ochefu said. "It was very bumpy."

Wright saw what was happening, recognizing that Ochefu needed someone to shepherd him along, and intentionally paired him with Mouphtou Yarou. Yarou had been through the dismal times, through the years where Villanova lost its way, and the 13–19 season when things hit rock bottom. He had watched a team too concerned with its individual achievements mess up its chemistry and he, along with senior teammate James "Tahj" Bell, were determined to right it by showing, instead of just telling, the freshmen what to do. When it was time to lift, the seniors would show up early. When it was time to practice, they went the hardest, determined to win every drill.

Yarou, too, is from Africa—he grew up in Benin, West Africa—and he and Ochefu could share the unique cultural experiences they'd had growing up. It also didn't hurt that both loved to play FIFA video games. The two roomed together that first year and, though a senior, Yarou never thought helping Ochefu was a burden. Instead it was his way of paying it forward, doing for Ochefu what older players had down for him.

"I told Daniel and the other freshmen to just play hard, play defense, and no matter what keep a great attitude because that's what Coach Wright wants the freshman class to learn to do," said Yarou, who plays professionally in France.

Yarou helped, but Ochefu's transition wasn't easy. As a freshman, and serving as Yarou's backup, he averaged 17.5 minutes per game, pulling in 4.1 rebounds. But his offense lagged far behind—he scored just 3.5 points a game—and Ochefu struggled with his limited role.

"It's hard, especially coming out of high school where you've been the best player forever," Ochefu said. "All of a sudden, they're asking you to play 15 minutes and just be a rebounder. That's not easy."

Elizabeth Ochefu, no shrinking violet, noticed her son's struggles and brought it to the attention of the coaching staff. Wright laughingly remembers Elizabeth sitting in his office with his assistants, pointing at each of them saying, "You and you and you are not working." She'd then grab a box score, note how many points Villanova had scored in the game, and then how few her son had contributed.

When Ochefu signed with Villanova, Elizabeth, with her poetic flare for speech, told Wright she was giving him a rock. She expected him to return a diamond. In that first season, she wasn't so certain Wright was cutting the rock properly.

"I didn't call him. I met with him," she said. "I always challenged him and he always reminded me that he had over 29 years of experience basketball wise. It took me time to realize it, but he knows exactly how to handle things, how to mix the right measure of discipline with the right measure of encouragement. He knew exactly what to do for my child."

But like his mother, Ochefu didn't see that immediately, either. He was perhaps even more frustrated than Elizabeth, and though he tried to let his aggravation fuel him, at times it overwhelmed him. When he felt like he was out of balance, Ochefu turned to a familiar face.

As he promised during Ochefu's recruiting visit, Hagan kept his door open to any players who wanted to talk, and Ochefu frequently took him up on the offer. With his position in athletics, Hagan was familiar enough with Ochefu's basketball career to understand what was going on, but as a priest and someone removed from the coaching staff, detached enough to offer an outsider's perspective. He counseled Ochefu on what he called the grace to persevere, introducing him to the parable of the barren fig tree. In the story, a vineyard owner tells his gardener to cut down the tree that has yet to bear fruit. The gardener asks for time, to allow him one more year to tend to the tree.

"For a freshman, everything doesn't happen as fast as they'd like to see it happen," Hagan said. "We'd have great conversations about hanging in there, about tapping the rock. This on-demand generation, these guys can dial up everything, microwave it in 30 seconds. Nobody wants to wait for anything. I told him the parable, that the gardener said, 'Let me cultivate the soil, pull out the weeds, and the rocks.' He knew it might not bear fruit for a few years, but he trusted that it would one day. That's what I told Daniel. Trust it."

The priest's message echoed Wright's common refrain—"trust the process." Reluctantly, Ochefu did. He went to the gym in his free time, working independently just as he did as a high school player to get better. His defensive skills, his rebounding, he knew were solid and college ready, so he concentrated on his shooting form. It was agonizingly boring work, essentially taking shot after shot, completing drill after drill, but in increments Ochefu started to see his efforts bear fruit.

At the end of his sophomore year, Ochefu, along with teammate Darrun Hilliard, were named the Big East Conference's Most Improved Players. That season, Ochefu averaged 5.7 points and 6.1 rebounds per game, tying JayVaughn Pinkston and James Bell as the team's leading rebounder.

And then things took off. "I saw it click," Berger said. As a junior, Ochefu earned honorable mention All–Big East honors, and ranked eighth at Villanova in blocked shots in a career—he blocked five in one game alone. That year he nearly doubled his scoring, averaging 9.2 points per game to go along with 8.5 rebounds. More important, Ochefu became a more reliable player and scorer. In the first 11 games of his junior season, Ochefu turned the ball over 26 times; in the last 11, just 16.

And the same player who shot just 46 percent from the floor and 48 percent from the free-throw line as a freshman led the Big East in field-goal percentage as a junior, connecting on 64 percent of his shots, and hit 69 percent of his free throws.

"When you have a big guy like that, everybody tells you, 'You gotta get it to the big guy. You gotta get it to the big guy,' and the big guy tells you that, too," Wright said. "But if you go to the big guy and he turns the ball over sometimes, and when he gets fouled, he makes one out of two, it's not efficient. You go to the big guys and they don't turn the ball over and they shoot a high percentage, and they make free throws, that's when it's really valuable. It's taken [Daniel] three years to get to that point."

Ochefu still texted Berger regularly, usually after a game. But now he simply wanted to know what his old coach saw in his game. There were no more requests to meet, no phone calls or desperate conversations. "There was nothing else going on. He was on the same page with Jay," Berger said.

Ochefu recorded three double-doubles in the first three games of his senior year, and six in the Wildcats' first 15. Against Seton Hall, he connected on 6-of-13 from the floor and 8-of-10 from the line to score 20 points, and pulled down 18 rebounds. If a four-year senior can have a breakout game, that was it for Ochefu.

As good as Ochefu was, though, at that point in the season the Wildcats were living up to their old moniker as Guard U. They relied heavily on a team stocked with terrific outside shooters to blaze to a 13–2 record. Even with Ochefu's increased production, in those first 15 games nearly half of Villanova's shot attempts came from beyond the three-point arc.

Four out, one in, they called the offense, which almost implied that Ochefu—the one in—was also left out. Once, as a freshman and maybe even as a sophomore, Ochefu might have seen it that way, too. But over time, as he first learned to understand Wright and then understood what the coach was teaching, Ochefu realized that a player could impact a game in other ways than just scoring. Lost in the rebounding and scoring statistics from those first 15 games is an equally critical number—the 22 assists Ochefu dished out.

"From the time bigs are in the second grade until they exit the NBA, they're constantly frustrated about not getting the ball enough," Berger said. "And with Villanova, a team that shoots such a high percentage of three-pointers, Daniel was getting the ball even less. And he knew, getting the ball less and less, he was showing the NBA guys less of what he can do. Not once did he complain about it. It was 'whatever this team needs.' It was so refreshing."

His mother saw the change in her son, too. She saw a boy who always had a big personality but often preferred to blend in emerging as a vocal leader for his team and she watched as her son, the same child who always questioned authority, started to accept and welcome discipline.

"My father always said to me, 'A wise person learns from other peoples' mistakes, but a fool learns from his own mistakes.' Daniel didn't want to be in that position of being a fool," Elizabeth said.

But Ochefu, who spent four years learning the value of perseverance from Hagan, would have to endure more lessons on the topic before finishing his Villanova career. At the end of January, he suffered a concussion in practice, sidelining him for three games; a month later, in the Wildcats' next-to-last game of the regular season, at home against DePaul, Ochefu rolled his ankle. The injury was significant—he played just 23 minutes and took only one shot against the Blue Demons—and came at a critical juncture for the team and for Ochefu.

He was able to play in the regular-season finale against Georgetown, but days later tweaked the injury in practice—and right before Villanova, the Big East regular-season champions, were about to play in the Big East Tournament.

A little bit stubborn and a lot of bit determined, Ochefu insisted on trying to play in Villanova's quarterfinal game against Georgetown. Clearly limited and at times hobbling up the court, he lasted just 13 ineffective minutes, missing his only two shots, failing to corral even a single rebound.

A game-time decision for the semifinal against Providence, Ochefu played sparingly in the first half but as Providence rallied, cutting a onetime 14-point Villanova lead to just two, Wright told his team to exploit Ochefu's height advantage. With the ankle injury clearly hurting him, Ochefu scored eight points in 15 minutes, but all eight came in a pivotal three-minute stretch when the senior all but single-handedly lifted the Wildcats to the win and into the Big East Tournament final against Seton Hall.

The game epitomized who Ochefu had become in his four years at Villanova, and just how important he was to the team's success.

"That's our leader," Josh Hart said after the game. "That's who we're going to live and die with. To see him get out there, obviously on a hurt ankle, but just for him to get out there and give us every-thing he has, it just shows how much of a leader he is. How bought-in he is. He doesn't care about stats, averages, points, rebounds, any-thing like that. He cares about the success of this team and that's what he showed. Came in, bum leg, and gave us everything he had."

Turned out that was the truth, almost literally. In the title game, Ochefu could only muster five points in 19 minutes of play and was clearly limited, unable to connect on his usually reliable jumpers or even launch off his balky ankle to dunk the ball. Not coincidentally, Villanova lost the Big East Tournament championship to Seton Hall.

Suddenly the status of the player many viewed as an after-thought—the odd man out in Villanova's guard-centric system—was the Wildcats' most pressing issue.

He would spend most of the five days off between the Seton Hall loss and the first-round NCAA Tournament game against UNC Asheville in the training room with athletic trainer Jeff Pierce, only returning to practice in full the day before the Wildcats' NCAA opening game in Brooklyn.

Wright decreed him ready in the press conference before the game against Asheville and Ochefu echoed his coach's faith, saying he felt fine.

"I'm feeling good. I'm feeling ready to go," Ochefu said before the game.

Against UNC Asheville, a team that didn't have a player taller than 6-foot-6 on its roster, Ochefu indeed proved ready to go. He scored a team-high 17 points, pulled in 10 rebounds, blocked three shots, and assisted on four baskets in Villanova's 30-point rout.

No one would ask him about the ankle for the rest of the NCAA Tournament. Ochefu would continue to play his role on the court as an opportunistic scorer (he'd score 17 in the regional semifinal against

Miami) who typically found other ways to contribute. Against Iowa, he'd dish out four assists, block three shots, and collect three steals; in the Kansas game, he'd pull down eight rebounds.

"Be the best street sweeper you can be."

That's how George Halcovage, Villanova's director of basketball operations, would describe Villanova's mindset after the national championship game. Wright wanted a team of players who thought no job was beneath them, that if they were asked to simply clean up the court they'd do it with the same precision and energy as the guy asked to score all the points.

Ochefu, maybe more than anyone on the team, came to embody that attitude over the course of his four years. His position, coupled with the way Villanova traditionally played, meant he'd never be the obvious star. He'd have his moments—a career-high 25-point night against St. John's, only days after returning from the concussion—but to outsiders who merely judged a player's worth by his scoring output, Ochefu would always appear to be a role player.

Wright, the Wildcats, and everyone associated with Villanova knew otherwise.

"He's the guy," Wright said simply. "He's the guy making all the communication out there. He's the guy that can guard multiple positions. He's a hell of a player, man. He is a very talented, underrated player, I believe."

Still, the irony wasn't lost on anyone that, in the final moments before Villanova's most critical play, Ochefu quite literally became an expert street sweeper. Except just like the people who misinterpret Ochefu's value based solely on his scoring, those who thought he was just having a little fun got it all wrong.

To run that final play properly, it's up to Ochefu to set a hard screen that allows Arcidiacono to cut inside and toward the center of the court. He'd have to set that screen in the exact place where he'd slid out of bounds seconds earlier, leaving that skid mark of sweat. Ochefu watched the young boy charged with clean-up duty work the mop as he pointed to some wet marks. But the boy wasn't quite getting it, so Ochefu ever so politely asked if he could do it himself.

"I knew the little kid was having a hard time," Ochefu said after the game. "I knew exactly where I had to set the screen. I didn't want to slip. I didn't want Arch to slip. I'm the one that dove, so I left a big wet spot on it. So I was like, make sure the floor is dry."

Sitting in the stands in Houston, Berger, Ochefu's high school coach, couldn't help but smile. Tantamount among Westtown's guiding Quaker principles is that the school exists as one community, which means everyone has a job to do. Every student has a chore. Some might set the table, others might clean it up. The school believes the tasks teach both selflessness and the importance that one person can have on the whole.

That, Berger thought, is exactly what he saw Ochefu doing as he mopped the floor in the national championship game.

"To be truthful, that maybe was my proudest moment watching him in all of his four years at Villanova," Berger said. "I knew there had to be a good reason on the basketball side to it, but I also thought, *How many superstars are going to sit there and point to that 12-year-old or tell him he's not doing it right?* Daniel just said, 'No, I'll take care of it,' and did something so small but something so important for his whole team."

Elizabeth Ochefu didn't see any of it. She was too afraid to watch the last seconds of the game, and sat next to her husband with her hands over her eyes. She saw it later, when she watched the replay of the game. At first she laughed to herself.

"I thought, *Wow, Villanova has not only turned him into a man, but they turned him into a man who mops floors,*" she joked.

But as she thought about it more, about all her son had been through, she, like Berger, realized the gravitas of that small act. The Ochefus took their son to Nigeria in the hopes of teaching him to appreciate all that he had. They let him find his way at boarding school in the hopes that he would mature. They sent him to Villanova in the hopes that he would learn the value of teamwork.

And there, in front of more than 70,000 people and a national television audience as he mopped a floor, Daniel Ochefu proved he had become even more than his mother had hoped.

"There was thoughtfulness, that he could have fallen down or Ryan could have fallen," she said. "And there was the recognition that it was up to him to make sure everything was right. He was hungry for the win but in that there was humility, too. Hungry and humble—that is the essence of Villanova basketball."

The court at the Final Four looks like a boxing ring set up for a heavyweight fight, which in some ways, of course, it is. Plopped in the middle of what usually serves as a domed football field, it is surrounded on all four sides with fans, and elevated much like a stage. The NCAA opted to move out of smaller, more intimate arenas back in 1996, when the national organization realized it could attract crowds upward of 70,000 as opposed to just 30,000.

For the 2016 title game, 74,340 pushed through the turnstile.

Almost all of them were on their feet as Ryan Arcidiacono took the inbounds pass with 4.7 seconds left. They weren't silent, but they were muted, the noise more a murmur and nothing near a roar. It was as if everyone—North Carolina fanatics, Villanova die-hards, casual fans, corporate muckety mucks, reporters, ushers, vendors—was too overcome to make any noise. Inside the stadium it was quiet enough that you could hear the ball bounce. On the television feed, you could hear the squeak of sneakers.

After taking the inbounds pass from Kris Jenkins, Arcidiacono took two dribbles with his left hand as he sped up the court and past the North Carolina bench.

Once he hit Daniel Ochefu's screen, he crossed the ball over to his right hand and with just two more bounces traversed the halfcourt line.

He dribbled once more, and then ever so slightly, turned his head toward the right.

He heard Jenkins before he saw him.

"Even with 76,000 people in the place, once you're on the floor, its 94 by 50 feet and all you hear is each other," Arcidiacono said. "All I heard was, 'Arch, Arch, Arch.' Right as I got to halfcourt, Kris sprinted a little more to get in my vision."

Nova, the Wildcats' last-second play, includes plenty of nuances and even more variations, but one thing never changes—the ball is always in Arcidiacono's hands.

Jay Wright long ago dubbed his point guard "Mr. Villanova," a nod not just to Arcidiacono's love for the school but also to the way he epitomizes the program. At his very first practice in a Villanova uniform—and only 10 months removed from back surgery that cost him his senior season of high school—Arcidiacono, only 6-foot-3 and 195 pounds, was on defense when JayVaughn Pinkston, a 6-foot-7, 250-pound beast of a player, caught a head of steam and barreled down the lane.

Arcidiacono stepped in front of Pinkston, took the charge, and fell to the floor as if he'd been bulldozed. Within seconds, he popped back up and onto his feet, ready to play.

"We're thinking, *No one wants to take a charge from that guy. What's he doing?*" Wright said. "And then I said, 'Well, I guess he's alright.'"

As impressed as he was stunned, Wright named Arcidiacono—only a freshman—a team captain. He was the first rookie Wright trusted with the job.

Over and over, Arcidiacono rewarded his coach's faith. By the time he graduated, he had started in all but one game in his four years—ceding his starting spot on Senior Night festivities during his sophomore year, allowing walk-on Nick McMahon to open in his place—and Villanova owned a 117–27 record, two Big East regular-season titles, one Big East Tournament crown, and, of course, one national championship.

And the kid cursed with a mouthful of an Italian surname (it's produced "Archie-dee-ah-cano") had become so popular, he was more than just a household name. He was a household nickname.

"Barack Obama is tough but Arcidiacono, man, that's a lot of vowels, so we're just going to call him Arch," President Obama said during the team's White House visit.

It all reads like a screenplay for a Disney movie, but one so perfect even the sappiest movie maker might call it too unbelievable.

Ryan Arcidiacono is the son of two Villanova graduates.

His father, Joe, grew up in a boisterous and athletic Italian family. Everyone played something in the extended Arcidiacono clan. (They still do, in fact. The current generation counts six kids on college rosters: two in lacrosse, two in football, one in baseball, and, of course, one in basketball.) Joe preferred hoops but soon realized his own broad frame was built more for football. He parlayed a solid high school career into a scholarship as an offensive tackle at Villanova, foreshadowing his son's future by earning his own spot as team captain in his senior season.

He met his wife, Patti, at college. She was from Long Island, and lived on the same dorm floor as Wright's future wife, Patty. The couple married, settling in Langhorne, Pennsylvania, just 40 minutes from the Villanova campus, and just seven miles from where Wright grew up. They had six kids (Sabrina, Nicole, Michael, Ryan, and twins, Courtney and Chris) and quickly fell into the typical parental taxicab life, shuttling their children from one event to the next.

At some point, a six-foot Fisher-Price basketball hoop showed up in the living room. It became a fixture.

Joe works as a pharmaceutical sales rep; Patti is a NICU nurse at a nearby hospital. As their kids grew up and headed off to college, they let them make their own choices, but secretly hoped one might opt for their own alma mater. Instead Sabrina, Michael, and Nicole chose Penn State—Nicole even played basketball there.

And then along came Ryan. When he took to that Fisher-Price hoop, he more often than not was mimicking a play of some Villanova player he'd just watched on TV. He was transfixed by the game and with the Wildcats.

Which came first, the love for hoops or the love for Villanova? Hard to know now, but ultimately one bled so thoroughly into the other they were one passion for Arcidiacono. He attended games with his dad and, as a local kid, could catch almost all of the Wildcats' schedule on television. He rarely missed a game.

Once, while his extended family vacationed at Woodloch Resorts in the Pocono Mountains, then 12-year-old Arcidiacono snuck off under the pretense of using the bathroom. A good 20 minutes later after Arcidiacono had yet to return, the family started to search the resort. They finally found him in the game room, in front of a television, oblivious to the worry he had caused. He was too busy watching No. 4 Villanova upset top-ranked UConn.

"I had the game circled on my calendar," Arcidiacono said by way of explanation. "I wasn't going to miss it."

In a state where so many kids—even three in his own house— grew up transfixed by Penn State football, Arcidiacono was a Villanova basketball die-hard.

"Him putting on a Villanova jersey is like a kid in Alabama putting on an Alabama football jersey," Wright has said.

So when, at the conclusion of one of Wright's summer camps, the coach pulled Arcidiacono and his father aside, suggesting that one day he, too, might bleed Villanova blue and white like his parents, the awestruck seventh-grader turned to his father in disbelief.

"Dad, was he being honest?"

"And I go, 'I think he was, Ry,'" Joe Arcidiacono said.

By then it was already obvious that Arcidiacono was special. He blitzed by everybody on the court, his talent only outmatched by his determination. His future high school coach, Jerry Devine, first spied Arcidiacono when Joe asked if his boy could join one of the high school workouts. Arcidiacono was easily the best player on the court.

He was in the eighth grade.

So it wasn't so much a decision as it was a logical march that led Arcidiacono to point his future toward basketball. Once a very good quarterback and decent catcher, he eventually hung up his shoulder pads and baseball mitt, turning his attention solely to basketball.

If he wasn't watching hoops, he was shooting hoops, pestering his pop to shoot with him or play pickup. Wanting only to feed his son's passion, Joe sought out every advantage he could find. He signed him up with the PA Playaz, a local summer-league team, and bought him special training equipment. He drove Arcidiacono to the nearby Newtown Athletic Club and even asked a wealthy buddy for the key to his house and indoor gym.

Eventually Joe realized his old-school game was no match for his son's abilities—"I played basketball 100 years ago, back with the three-man weave," Joe said—so he searched for a better trainer.

He found Ben Luber, a local kid who had starred at neighboring Council Rock High School. Now an assistant coach at Rider University, Luber at the time was working exclusively as a trainer.

Arcidiacono would work with Luber for two hours almost every day. The workouts were relentless, a barrage of drills to develop

Arcidiacono's ballhandling skills, shot, and foot speed. They'd work at dribbling the ball high and as low as mere inches off the ground; Arcidiacono would dribble with a ball in each hand, passing one at a time to Luber. The two would practice endless catch-and-shoot drills, moving Arcidiacono around the three-point arc and back again.

And then they'd come back the next day and do it all again.

Arcidiacono couldn't get enough. Most days when his father got home from work, his son would ask to find a court or available gym so they could practice more.

"I'd be like, 'Uh, you already shot 300 today, can we stay in?'" Joe said. "But he just had that drive."

The hard work not only paid off in the form of a very good high school career—Arcidiacono would lead Neshaminy High School to two state playoffs, and score more than 1,400 points—but also on the recruiting trail. Though he was unranked heading into his sophomore year of high school, people were starting to hear about the kid from the Philadelphia suburbs and that fall, Arcidiacono was invited to attend Villanova's Hoops Mania, the Wildcats' annual preseason tipoff.

Arcidiacono couldn't believe it. It was as if Wright's promise that he, too, could bleed blue and white was coming true. This was in 2009, just six months after Villanova played in the Final Four. The program had never been hotter, attracting high-caliber recruits and a national buzz.

And Wright, who had orchestrated the Wildcats all the way back to national prominence, was even bigger.

The coach always commands a room. Joe jokingly likened him to the Pope. Everyone wants just a few seconds with Wright wherever he goes and the good-natured coach never says no. He stops for pictures, a quick chat, making sure everyone feels like they are the most important person in the room.

That night during Hoops Mania, Arcidiacono was one of several recruits in attendance, mostly local kids, including Amile Jefferson, who would go on to play at Duke, and Savon Goodman, who recently transferred from Arizona to La Salle.

Each family sat at a hightop table and Wright worked the room, greeting everyone warmly.

Everyone, that is, except the Arcidiaconos.

Wright never once came by their table.

As the minutes stretched on and the Arcidiaconos still waited for their time with Wright, they felt the room shrinking.

"I was like, 'Should we just leave or something?'" Arcidiacono said. "It was really awkward."

Now the family knows it was a simple oversight, of Wright being stretched too thin and completely unaware that he had missed their table.

But then it felt like more than just a slight. It felt like a cold bucket of water killing the entire family's dream. When director of basketball operations Jason Donnelly asked how the family's visit went, Arcidiacono sheepishly admitted he hadn't even said hello to the coach.

As the family walked back to the car, Joe put his arm around his son. Both equally heartbroken, he tried to sound the right note of encouragement.

"Hey, Ry, this probably isn't the place for you but that's okay. We're going to find the right place for you," he said.

Joe believed it, but it devastated him and his wife as much as it did their son. The three of them rode the entire way home in silence.

Wright, for his part, doesn't even remember the incident, though he's since been ribbed repeatedly by both Joe and Arcidiacono.

As strange as it might sound, as a local kid Arcidiacono almost had a more difficult fight with the local school. He was from the suburbs not the city, and people naturally questioned just how good he was. Was he truly talented or just the beneficiary of subpar competition?

And more, Wright knew that to take a local kid it absolutely had to work. If he took Arcidiacono but never played him, Wright would lose face in the community and perhaps even trust with area coaches.

Wright talked frequently to his brother, Derek, about Arcidiacono. Younger by 13 years, Derek Wright is a high school coach at Council Rock South (Wright's high school split 13 years ago into North and South). The Arcidiaconos live just on the other side—or wrong side, in Derek's mind—of the district line. A few more feet and Ryan might have played for one Wright in high school and another in college. Derek jokingly suggested more than once that the Arcidiaconos ought to consider moving.

Arcidiacono was a middle-schooler the first time Derek saw him play, suiting up for St. Andrew's, the parish school nearby. He loved the kid immediately, struck by his on-court intelligence and, of course, his toughness. But Derek also understood his brother's reluctance.

"He thought if he was going to recruit this kid and he was coming because of his connection to Villanova and he's from my area, if it doesn't work, it's not going to be good in a lot of ways," Derek said.

The relationship, Wright recognized, had to work on both sides.

Of course, it would have helped if it had simply gotten started.

Instead, with that sting of rejection still fresh, Arcidiacono reluctantly broadened his horizons. He never fully gave up on Villanova but he figured his dad might be right, that as much as he dreamed of becoming a Wildcat, maybe there was someplace else that he truly belonged.

And just as he opened his eyes to new opportunities, his game blossomed. By the end of his sophomore year, Arcidiacono went from an unranked player to one rated 33rd in the ESPN 60 rankings. Coaches liked his talent; they loved his determination. In one summer-league game, Arcidiacono took a nasty, face-first spill on the court, slicing open his forehead and covering the gym floor with blood. Eight stitches later, he not only persuaded his parents to let him play; he scored 35 points.

Pretty soon Kansas' Bill Self, Notre Dame's Mike Brey, and Florida's Billy Donovan were learning how to pronounce "Arcidiacono," gauging his interest in their respective schools.

Donovan, coming off back-to-back national championships just three years before, grew especially enamored with the feisty point guard. He'd heard about Arcidiacono threw the small-world circles of basketball. Gene Rice, Arcidiacono's summer-league coach, is from the same Long Island town that Donovan once called home, and though older, he knew Donovan from a distance. Rice suggested the coach might appreciate the way Arcidiacono played, so Donovan made a trip to watch him play.

He was impressed with Arcidiacono's skills, his ballhandling and toughness, but it was an off-court evaluation that really sold the coach. Donovan watched Arcidiacono in a September conditioning workout with his high school teammates.

"Ryan had an unbelievable threshold for pain," said Donovan, now the Oklahoma City Thunder coach. "He could push himself beyond his limits. When you get a guy like that, athleticism becomes a wash because whatever he might have lacked, he overcame it with work ethic."

That's how Donovan built his own career at Providence, pushing the Friars to the 1987 Final Four with his will as much as his talent, so Arcidiacono's doggedness was especially appealing. With few schools really showing much interest in Arcidiacono, Donovan decided to make him a priority.

For weeks in a row Arcidiacono would show up at his high school at 5:45 in the morning for a before-school workout only to find Donovan had beaten him there.

Other coaches—including Wright—certainly were interested, but no one else made the pre-dawn practices. Donovan's devotion did not go unnoticed by Arcidiacono, especially after being ignored earlier by Wright.

"I don't want to throw Coach Wright under the bus, but Villanova is so close to Neshaminy, I kept wondering, *Why isn't Coach Wright doing this? Does he not want me anymore?*" Arcidiacono said. "I think what happened to me earlier gave me more of an open mind and so when Villanova offered, I was like, 'Okay, thank you, but I have other offers, too.'"

Eventually Arcidiacono boiled his choices down to Villanova, his old love, and Florida, his newfound flame. Already familiar with Villanova, he chose to visit Florida first. The Gators turned on the dog-and-pony show for their hot recruit. They feted Arcidiacono and his parents at a football game, bringing them on the field and introducing him to former Gators turned pro athletes. As he walked to his seat in the stands, fans chanted, "Gator basketball! Gator basketball!" at him.

They showed him around their state-of-the-art practice facility and broke down films, showing Arcidiacono exactly how he'd fit into the Gators offense. It was heady stuff for a teenager and, coupled with Donovan's regular appearances at the high school gym, turned Arcidiacono's head completely.

That evening, Donovan and his staff took Joe and Patti out to dinner while their son visited with the players.

"I'm sitting there peeking at the television because the Phillies were in the World Series," Joe said. "Patti was twisting and tearing up bar napkins because she thinks she's losing her son to Florida and not Villanova."

Donovan sensed the turmoil with the family, going so far as to tell Joe he'd pull out of recruiting Arcidiacono if it was causing too much upset within the family. But Arcidiacono stood his ground, attracted to Florida because, quite simply, the coaches were paying more attention to him than Villanova.

The family had barely left campus when Arcidiacono announced he was calling Donovan to commit to the University of Florida. Crushed and slightly panicked, Patti and Joe asked that their son at least finish visiting other schools. He'd already arranged travel plans to Notre Dame, Boston College, and, later that same week, was scheduled to go to Villanova.

In the backseat, Arcidiacono listened but in his mind, he was merely humoring them. He was going to Florida. They drove to the airport in silence.

By the time the family flew from Gainesville to Philadelphia, Arcidiacono hadn't changed his mind. He was hell-bent on becoming a Gator and when he walked through the door at the family's home, declared his intention. "I'm going to Florida!" he yelled.

His oldest sister, Sabrina, started crying.

"Sobbing, actually," Arcidiacono said.

Arcidiacono is the fourth of the six kids and Sabrina, older by eight years, is like a second mom. She already was out of college when he was in high school, so she was around to attend his games and listen to his problems. The two are extraordinarily close.

Already engaged at the time and teaching at a nearby high school, Sabrina sobbed that her brother wouldn't be around when she had children, that she would no longer be able to watch him play if he went all the way to Florida.

"I was kind of like, 'Oh well, at least they really love me,'" Arcidiacono said. "But it didn't change my mind."

That was on a Tuesday.

On Wednesday, Arcidiacono was scheduled to attend Villanova's Hoops Mania, the same event Wright had ignored him at just a year earlier.

Patti Arcidiacono persuaded her reluctant son to at least promise to give Villanova a chance, and not make any phone calls or commitments until he finished that visit.

In the meantime, she used the 24 hours to work the phones, convincing all of Arcidiacono's siblings to attend the visit with him. "I think she and Jay were in cahoots with a plan," Joe said.

Indeed this time, Wright made sure to visit extensively with Arcidiacono.

Childhood dreams are hard to kill, especially ones that course not just through a person's veins but through his very DNA. Now fully embraced by the Villanova community and surrounded by his own Villanova family, Arcidiacono quickly forgot why he ever loved another school.

"We weren't even halfway through the night and I realized, okay, this is the spot for me," Arcidiacono said. "I loved the place. It felt like home."

Just as they did the year before, the family piled into the Dodge Caravan to head east on the Pennsylvania Turnpike, toward home.

Only this time instead of silence and heartbreak, Arcidiacono made his family's day when he announced he had changed his mind. He wasn't going to Florida.

He was going to be a Villanova Wildcat.

"I think I had barely said the word 'Villanova' and my dad was dialing Coach Wright's phone number and handing me the phone," Arcidiacono said.

Ironically, Wright didn't answer. He was with his coaches, celebrating the end of Hoops Mania. Arcidiacono left a voice message, promising he'd call the next day but he didn't say what he was calling about. When he finally did reach Wright, the coach was leaving an area golf course to pick up his daughter, Reilly, from basketball practice.

Concerned about losing cell reception, he pulled over and spent 45 minutes talking to Arcidiacono—leaving his daughter waiting. When Wright finally arrived, Reilly was in her coach's car in the school parking lot, Wright's wife was furious (she'd been texting him while he was on the phone), but the coach and Arcidiacono were giddy.

Donovan was understandably disappointed when Arcidiacono called to say he'd changed his mind, but even he understood.

"Once Jay got involved and Ryan realized he really did want him, Ryan was so much more at peace," he said. "I never felt like his arm was twisted at all. He's got terrific parents and I think they were just worried about him going so far away. I completely understood it all. He ended up at the right place."

The weighty decision off his shoulders, Arcidiacono pointed forward to what he figured—and hoped—would be an easy future for him, and for Villanova.

It was anything but.

The pain started somewhere during the winter, a shooting laser beam that ran down Ryan Arcidiacono's leg.

Naturally, he ignored it. As a lifelong athlete, he was accustomed to aches and pains and chalked this up to the typical wear and tear of constant basketball. He continued to play, even pushing through the summer showcase season, figuring it would eventually go away.

Instead, it got worse. He tried multiple cortisone shots, hoping they would do the trick.

No change.

Finally Arcidiacono went to see a doctor who recommended an immediate MRI.

This was in September of 2011, the beginning of his senior year, months before his final high school season.

The film came back showing a herniation between the L4 and L5 discs in his back. The injury required surgery and a lengthy recovery. Arcidiacono would miss the entirety of his final high school basketball season.

"I remember being more annoyed than scared," he said. "Just annoyed that I couldn't play basketball."

His parents were scared.

Again the trio piled in for another silent car ride, this time to consult with doctors in Philadelphia.

"It was so fundamentally wrong," Joe said. "We're driving down 95 to have someone talk to us about having our son's back operated on."

They met with Dr. Alex Vaccaro, a nationally renowned surgeon and the president of the Rothman Institute, a world leader in orthopedics. Impressed by his credentials and his vow that their son would recover as good as new, the family booked Arcidiacono's surgery for December 21, 2011.

After the surgery, Vaccaro declared the procedure went perfectly, but the long road back was just beginning. Arcidiacono, the same kid who spent hours working on ballhandling drills, couldn't do anything. For two weeks, he couldn't even ride in a car. He was allowed to take walks. That was it.

And so in December and January, with snow piling up around their neighborhood and the air cold enough they could see their breath, Joe would guide his son by the elbow, cautioning him to watch out for curbs and keep an eye out for turns in the walkway. Day after day, they shuffled along, the scene as gray and somber as their moods.

"It's like I'm holding a 60-year-old," Joe said. "I'm just standing there and I got a tear in my eye. I can't believe this has happened to this superstar, this great little kid."

Ever positive, Arcidiacono refused to wallow in self-pity. Instead of fretting over what he couldn't do, he embraced what he could. No longer committed to hours in the gym, he enjoyed just being a normal teenager again, using his newfound spare time to hang out with friends.

When he wasn't rehabbing—stretching and working in a pool, concentrating on strengthening his core to support his back—he naturally watched Villanova.

Unfortunately, that didn't offer much refuge.

Four days before Arcidiacono went under the knife, the Wildcats lost to city rival Saint Joseph's 74–58. On New Year's Day, they dropped to 7–7 following a loss to Marquette, the beginning of an unraveling that would end with a 13–19 record and Wright realizing he had to reconstruct his team again.

Sitting in his family room, Arcidiacono never wavered in his commitment to Villanova. On the contrary, the struggling season only reaffirmed he was making the right decision. It wasn't about playing time—though certainly he figured he could get some minutes—it was about what the fiery guard saw as a challenge.

"I kept thinking, *Okay, what can I do to help my team win?*" he said. "I don't mean I need to come in and score a million points. What do they need me to do? How can I help fix this?"

The public answer came four years later, in the national championship game.

But Arcidiacono offered a private, more critical answer as soon as he stepped on campus. In taking that charge against teammate JayVaughn Pinkston—his back still recovering, his speed admittedly nowhere near where it normally would be—he defined how Villanova would play.

This would be a team that would not worry about the future, but instead would play in the present. It would not define itself by outsiders' evaluations and expectations, or even by a final record. It would be about how it played.

"We've always talked about that every single year, but this group lived it," Wright said. "Making a goal doesn't get it done. Your commitment is what gets it done. This group understood that."

Beginning with Arcidiacono's first game, in which he played 28 minutes, Wright quite literally couldn't afford to take his guard off the floor. He was more than indispensable, he was an extension of the coach himself. He knew what Wright needed or wanted before the coach even said it, the connection between the two so strong, Arcidiacono's teammates jokingly called him Wright's son.

In his four years, Arcidiacono never finished a season as the team's leading scorer but in each, he led the Wildcats in minutes played and assists.

And not coincidentally, as the way Arcidiacono played defined the way Villanova played, the team got better and better with each passing year.

It wasn't easy. He and Daniel Ochefu bear the scars of the labor—a 22-point loss in New York to Alabama followed by an 18-point home loss to Columbia during their freshman season; the latter rightly earning the Wildcats a few boos from the fans.

But they pushed forward undaunted, a 20-win season leading to a 29-win season leading to a 33-win season.

And of course, one first-weekend NCAA Tournament loss (to North Carolina) begetting another first-weekend NCAA Tournament loss (to UConn) begetting yet another first-weekend NCAA Tournament loss (N.C. State).

Arcidiacono watched as various seniors—James Bell, Tony Chennault, Darrun Hilliard, and JayVaughn Pinkston—sobbed their way out of the locker room at the end of their season.

He knew in 2015–16 that very well could be him.

"I say it now that I'm not going to worry about it," Arcidiacono said before his senior season began, "but I also know it's my last one."

For the most part, the last one went almost seamlessly. Villanova lost just five regular-season games, even ascending to the program's first No. 1 ranking, in February.

Critics questioned whether the Wildcats were merely No. 1 by default—they were the sixth team to grab the top spot—but they also held their position for three weeks, ceding it only after losing at Xavier.

By the time Villanova headed to New York for the Big East Tournament, the Wildcats were rolling with a head of steam, winning three in a row and 10 of their final 11 regular-season games. They throttled Georgetown in the first game of the conference tourney, dispatched of Providence in the semifinals, and then squared up against Seton Hall for the title.

At halftime, Villanova trailed the Pirates by 11. Seton Hall was the aggressor, putting up 40 points against a Wildcats team that allowed just 63.6 per game. When Arcidiacono's last prayer of a three-pointer fell short, giving Seton Hall the league tournament crown, more than a few folks figured Villanova was headed back to its postseason troubles.

Even Arcidiacono's own family wondered when the joyride would end. They drove to the first-weekend NCAA Tournament games in Brooklyn and made the 10-hour road trip to Louisville—all of the kids except Sabrina—crammed in the family minivan.

And in the seconds before each game, as he watched his son warm up, as the final strands of the national anthem played and Villanova headed out for the opening tip, Joe Arcidiacono heard the same thoughts rattling around in his head.

Is this Ryan's last game? Is this his last time wearing a white jersey?

Only it never was. The answer to the critics and even Joe's curiosity came with one exclamation point after the other—a 30-point win against UNC Asheville and a 19-point win against Iowa to erase the first-weekend demons; a 23-point win against Miami and a five-point win against Kansas to earn the Final Four ticket.

When the Arcidiaconos got home from their road trip to Louisville, Joe walked into his son's room. Years ago, back when Ryan was in grade school, he persuaded his dad to bid on an item at a silent auction of sports memorabilia. The money would go to a local charity, so Joe ponied up the bucks and won the autographed jersey his son had selected.

"It's a No. 1 Kansas jersey, signed by Bill Self," Joe laughed. "It's still in his room and that's who he just beat to get to the Final Four. It's hilarious."

In the six NCAA Tournament games, Arcidiacono would play 193 of a possible 240 minutes, earning the most rest in the 44-point blowout against Oklahoma. He'd turn the ball over only nine times and score 95 points.

In the Final Four he did not score the most points (he had 31 in two games to Josh Hart's 35 and Kris Jenkins' 32). He did not hit the game winner.

Yet when the Most Outstanding Player award was announced, he was the winner.

Why Arcidiacono won the award, and really why Villanova won the national title, explains everything about who he had been his entire life and how he had played in his four years at Villanova.

He made the most extraordinary play of the entire NCAA Tournament, or perhaps more appropriately, the most out of the ordinary play.

And it wasn't a basket. It was a pass.

As the Villanova players huddled around Wright in that final timeout, 4.7 seconds showing on the clock, Daniel Ochefu caught his classmate's eye. The Redemption Class brothers, their relationship forged as much on failure as success, knew how the play would go. The only question was how it would finish.

"I mouthed to [Ryan], 'Shoot it,'" Ochefu said.

It was a logical suggestion. Who else could possibly be better suited to take that shot?

This was a moment generations in the making, stretching back to two parents meeting on the Villanova campus, one a football star, the other a future nurse, who fell so hard for their college they dreamed their children might go there; to six kids, the first three all becoming Penn Staters instead but a fourth drinking the blue and white Kool-Aid, falling in love with Villanova; to a living room and a Fisher-Price hoop and hours of driveway games and training sessions; to a disappointed car ride home from a first Villanova recruiting visit; to a detour toward the University of Florida; to a giddy car ride home from a second Villanova recruiting trip; to back surgery; to regular-season accomplishment and postseason failure; to this, possibly the last 4.7 seconds of a kid's career.

Yet with the ball in his hands and the national championship on the line, Arcidiacono made the play that no one would expect.

He passed the ball, flipping an underhand toss to Jenkins before quickly scurrying away to give his teammate an open look at the basket.

"That's supposed to be his shot," Jenkins said after the game. "But he passed it to me."

Except Jenkins wasn't really surprised. No one who knows Arcidiacono was.

"For that play to work, you have to have a guy that you trust to make the right decision, to not be selfish and want to be the star himself," Wright said. "That's Ryan."

Added Joe Arcidiacono, "That play completely encapsulated his four years there."

Just a few weeks earlier, right before the Big East Tournament began, Wright met up with his brother at a local Dunkin Donuts. They talked about the upcoming games, the season, and the team. As Wright started to speak about Arcidiacono, Derek noticed his brother, usually a pro at hiding his emotions, choke up.

"I don't know what I'm going to do without him," Wright said.

For four years, Arcidiacono had lived the message Wright preached, fulfilling the coach's image of how his team could be reconstructed after everything had gone terribly wrong. More than that, Arcidiacono believed in the message. He believed that the process was important, that if a person did the right thing and behaved the right way, eventually the results would come. He held onto it through a difficult freshman season and three years of disappointing first-weekend postseason losses. When critics questioned Villanova's character and ability, Arcidiacono publicly accepted the criticism and privately vowed to get better.

He was Mr. Villanova, and never more so than on his final play in a Villanova uniform, when instead of taking a chance at being the hero, he set up his teammate to become a legend.

"That's Arch," Wright said after the game. "That doesn't surprise me at all. That's who he is. That's why we are who we are."

She watched his feet.

She knew the form of his shot would be masterful. She was certain the follow-through would be so flawless it would look as though he was posing for a picture.

What Felicia Jenkins didn't know was whether her son, launching from two steps beyond the three-point line, would get a good enough push to send the ball the extra distance.

And so while some people covered their eyes and others peeked through splayed fingers, while some refused to blink for fear of missing the outcome and some refused to watch in fear of seeing it, Felicia Jenkins did the strangest thing of all.

She looked down at Kris Jenkins' feet.

"I wanted to see the leg action on the floor," Felicia said. "To make sure he had enough leg strength."

In due time Felicia Jenkins, mother, would take over and practically mow people over as she tried to get to the court and hug her boy.

But before all that, before the confetti rained down from the ceiling and the players collapsed in a joyful scrum on the floor, Felicia Jenkins, coach, made a split-second assessment and found what she was looking for. When she saw her son's feet she was certain, maybe more certain than anyone other than Jenkins himself, that the ball was going in the basket.

"Good clean pass, hit him square in the hands, and he was leaning forward, so I knew he had the leg strength," she said. "So I knew. I knew."

If anyone should know how the final shot of the 2016 national championship game would play out, it is Felicia. An all-conference college player who later earned Hall of Fame distinction at her alma mater, and a successful high school and collegiate coach, she also is the architect of Jenkins' shot. Fox Sports analyst Gus Johnson dubbed Jenkins "Big Smoove," a nickname that played off his stocky frame, his cool demeanor, and that surefooted shot.

Felicia gave birth to Jenkins. She also gave rise to Big Smoove.

When every other kid was practicing highlight-film shots and launching three-pointers well out of reach, Jenkins was inside the three-point line, taking ordinary jumpers, sometimes even practicing old-school bank shots. Other kids tried to dunk. Jenkins perfected his layup. He hated it. He wanted to be like the other kids, going for the style points and perfecting his hero shot. Felicia wouldn't let him. In fact, the more he balked at the monotony of the basics, the more his mother insisted he practice.

From her own playing days at Division II Claflin University in South Carolina, Felicia knew that being a good basketball player wasn't about making impressive shots; it was about simply making shots. And so she schooled Jenkins in footwork and on repetition, turning his shot into a work of art and a fluid act of pure muscle memory. He didn't realize it, and took his own sweet time appreciating it, but Felicia was giving Jenkins the biggest arrow a shooter can have in his quiver—confidence.

"Kris Jenkins is the type of guy, and I mean this in the most complimentary way possible, he's a cocky shooter," Villanova associate head coach Baker Dunleavy said. "He came to Villanova expecting that this was going to happen to him. He was going to make a game-winning shot in a national championship."

The beautiful irony is Jenkins did exactly that only because his mother insisted he work on the fundamentals. Those fundamentals bred the confidence that allowed Jenkins, on the night of April 4, 2016, to launch a shot that made him even more than the hero he dreamed of being. It made him a legend. Christian Laettner, whose 1992 buzzer beater long stood as the defining moment of the NCAA Tournament, tweeted a picture to Jenkins in the aftermath of the championship game showing Jenkins wearing a crown. "Passing the torch," the Duke star wrote.

And it is all because mother knew best.

"If I had known it was all going to end this way, oh my goodness, I would have documented every step," Felicia said. "I didn't. I just firmly believed I was doing the right thing."

Doing the right thing, though, is not always the easy thing. That was certainly the case for the Jenkins family.

A basketball coach's life isn't always easy, not on the coach and certainly not on the coach's family. The lucky ones, the exceptions, hold onto the same position for years. The vast majority, especially those whose dreams are larger than high school courts, jump from one place to the next, hoping a ladder that often zigs and zags horizontally eventually will take on a vertical trajectory. Their families, sometimes willingly and sometimes grudgingly, go along for the ride.

Felicia Jenkins landed her first job in 1993, the same year her son and eldest child was born. She was named head coach at her high school alma mater, Eau Claire High School in Columbia, South Carolina. That quickly led to a spot at Orangeburg Consolidated District 4, in Felicia's hometown, which in turn four years later translated into a college assistant's position at her old stomping grounds, Claflin.

As Felicia's job opportunities grew, so did her son's own game. Buoyed by his mother's early teachings and blessed with her athleticism,

Jenkins played in summer-league showcases across the country, faring well enough to make a name for himself. As a 10-year-old, Jenkins and his teammates traveled to Florida, where they squared off against a Maryland-based team in the semifinals. Nate Britt Sr. was the team's coach; his son, Nate, one of the best players.

Britt Sr. spent 25 years as a detective with the Baltimore police department, seeing plenty of things he wishes he never had, losing too many friends in the line of duty.

A decent athlete himself and a lover of basketball, his job demanded enough of him that he had no intention of becoming a coach until his four-year-old son, Nate, decided to play soccer. The rec league didn't have enough coaches and asked Britt Sr. to fill in until they found someone.

Three years later, Britt Sr. had grown the squad into a travel team that finished undefeated.

"They never did find that replacement," he joked.

When Nate turned his attention to basketball, his father naturally took his whistle with him. He preached fundamentals and taught the boys basketball skills, but as a police officer, he also demanded discipline, lecturing them about behavior and sportsmanship as much as rebounding and dribbling.

More than the team's basketball prowess, the team's respectful attitude is what Felicia and her husband, Kelvin, noticed when the Britts' team played against Jenkins' squad in Florida. As the summer season wore on, Felicia and Kelvin made it a point to seek out Britt Sr. whenever their paths crossed.

If there are such things in life as fate and grand plans, the Jenkins family certainly believes in them. There is, frankly, no other way to explain the mixture of happenstance, tragedy, and opportunity that came together to yank one child away from what could have been a troubled path and turn him on a proper one.

To those who have heard the story, the Britts saved Jenkins.

Kris' sister, the one who never lived to see her first birthday, had something to do with it as well. Were it not for her, Jenkins might never have found the Britts.

Kori Jenkins was born on January 23, 2005, and doctors immediately realized something was wrong. She was diagnosed with DiGeorge syndrome, an autoimmune deficiency that can—and in Kori's case, did—affect the heart. By the time she was born, Felicia and Kelvin were struggling—they'd later divorce but remain a strong unit in their kids' lives—and Felicia, along with Kris and his two younger sisters, Kaiya and Kelci, were living in Baltimore with Felicia's sister.

Felicia understandably was preoccupied with Kori, who at first was treated at Mount Washington Hospital and later would have surgery at Johns Hopkins University Hospital. When she wasn't in the hospital, Felicia was at the nearby Ronald McDonald House. Desperate to keep Kris' mind occupied and his game sharp, she reached out to Britt Sr. to see if he remembered her boy from the previous year.

Britt Sr. has a special knack for recalling ballplayers—especially ones who played well against his team, and Jenkins had been very good. He remembered Kris immediately and invited him to come work out with his son. The two boys, speaking the communal language of basketball, immediately hit it off.

Soon a workout extended into a sleepover, a sleepover into a weekend, and, with little Kori still fighting for her life, a weekend eventually became the better part of the summer. Jenkins essentially moved in to the Britts' Upper Marlboro home and even played with Britt Sr.'s summer-league team.

"If Kori wasn't sick, I'd never have called the Britts," Felicia said. "There wouldn't have been a need, but I wanted Kris to have a chance to get away and play ball."

That fall Felicia moved back to South Carolina. In the midst of all the struggles, she had been awarded her dream—a head coaching job at Benedict College, a Division II school in Columbia. Kori transitioned first to the Children's Hospital there and eventually was able to come home.

Jenkins enrolled in a local middle school, the girls in an elementary school, and Felicia tried to juggle it all.

"I honestly don't know how I got through it all," she said. "Kris was young. My girls were young. I had to coach. It was very difficult."

She noticed little things at first. Jenkins, usually affable, was quieter. The boys he chose to hang out with at his new school weren't the same sort of crowd he'd gravitated toward before. His grades didn't plummet, but they slipped.

Felicia knew what she was seeing—a boy, still a child himself, trying to deal with too many adult problems.

And then it got even worse. On January 6, 2006, a little more than two weeks shy of her first birthday, Kori died at home. Felicia took a leave from coaching but there was no reprieve from her grief. There were days, she said, when she quite literally couldn't get out of bed. When she finally did, she didn't even recognize herself in the mirror because she had lost so much weight.

"Kris was dealing with all of that," she said.

The decision was made, not after an act of great defiance or disrespect but after Jenkins refused to turn over his cell phone when asked by a hall monitor at school. Felicia knew her boy and knew this was not like him.

Above all else, she knew she had to do something.

After consulting with Jenkins' father, Felicia picked up the phone and asked the Britts to take her eldest son again. Britt Sr. already had brought some structure into her son's life—Felicia noticed how, after living with the Britts for the bulk of the summer, Jenkins suddenly made his bed every day—and Britt Sr.'s wife, Melody, was all about academics. Their lives at the time, so much more structured and settled than her own, would be a haven.

The thought of losing another child, even by choice, even temporarily, was crushing, but Felicia couldn't come up with another solution.

"I never cried in front of him or my other kids," she said. "But I had my moments, in the shower, when I was driving alone, or in my 'me' time, but I knew I was doing the right thing."

Britt Sr. took the call and though he was taken aback, he wasn't stunned. He'd noticed things with Jenkins that summer, subtle things that made him think maybe he needed a little guidance. Britt Sr., for example, insisted his players end each game by shaking hands with the opposing coach, reminding them to offer a firm handshake and a sincere look in the eye. Jenkins thought the whole thing foolish, and though he did what he was told, his handshake was perfunctory, his gaze usually at his toes.

So when Felicia asked for help, he didn't hesitate. But he also knew the decision wasn't his alone. Having Jenkins in the house would impact everyone, so he convened a family meeting to discuss the arrangement. Britt Sr. worried his children might balk at sharing their parents—especially Nate, who spent so much time with his father in sports. Instead, Nate and his younger sister, Natayla, were immediately onboard with the idea.

Melody had the most reservations. She worried about their own family dynamic and even the financial burden of taking on another pre-teen. After much discussion, Britt Sr. finally looked his wife in the eye and asked her a simple question.

"Would you give up your son to somebody?" he said. "What would make you do that? [Melody] realized this was really a cry for a help and we decided if we can, let's help."

The Britts sat Jenkins down immediately, telling him that if he felt uncomfortable at any point he had to tell them. They joked that he couldn't simply try to pull their heartstrings to shirk household chores but that if he felt truly lonely or had any issues, he couldn't hesitate to tell him.

"He fell into our family like he'd been with us from day one," Britt Sr. said.

For Jenkins, the move wasn't altogether unsettling. Having lived with the Britts earlier, he was accustomed to them, their expectations and rules.

And Felicia didn't simply cut the cord and run. She stayed with him the first weekend and then made as many trips as her schedule would allow, bringing his sisters along with her. When she returned to South Carolina, she left notes behind for Jenkins to read so he'd have his mother's words even if he didn't have her voice all of the time.

The Britt home became the Jenkins' home, even for Felicia. She stayed over on the sofa or in Jenkins' room and thought nothing of folding the clothes, doing the laundry, or helping herself to what was in the refrigerator.

"They just welcomed me with open arms, so it was never uncomfortable," Felicia said. "I never felt like a visitor in their home."

For Jenkins, hanging with Nate offered immediate credibility with other kids in the neighborhood. And, if anyone questioned behind closed doors who the boy suddenly living with the Britts was, they never said or did anything publicly. Jenkins simply became part of the family, part of the community fabric.

At the time, no one thought it would be anything more than a temporary solution, a stopgap until Jenkins righted his path and Felicia felt secure enough to bring him home.

Instead, less than a year later and with the arrangement working so well for Jenkins, the two families stood before a judge and made the arrangement official. The Britts were named Jenkins' legal guardian until he graduated from high school.

In the legal execution, it sounds so simple—a hearing, a document, an adjournment, and guardianship is granted. In reality, it is a tricky and potentially rocky road to traverse. It only worked so easily for Jenkins because everyone was willing to make it work.

Felicia and Kelvin ceded everyday decisions to the Britts, the "parents" on site, and honored those choices.

The Britts treated Jenkins no differently than their own kids. He had chores to do and expectations to meet. If he wrote a paper that wasn't up to Melody's standards (and, most everyone agrees, those are pretty high standards), she sent him back for a major rewrite just as she would Nate or Natayla.

Nate and Natayla, meantime, willingly shared their own parents, and made room for another "brother" without a hint of jealousy.

"These people, these open-hearted, wonderful people, made it work," Felicia said.

And then there was Jenkins, blessed with two sets of parents but living apart from the family that raised him. His mother marvels at his strength. People, she said, like to talk about her sacrifice. They neglect, she believes, to appreciate his.

In the summer of 2006, for example, the adults agreed that Jenkins would be better served switching from the local public school to Mater Dei, the private middle school that Nate attended. The move meant Jenkins would have to repeat the seventh grade and spend the summer taking classes and working with a tutor.

He didn't love it. He called his mother, telling her he wasn't sure he could manage it. But she stood her ground and Jenkins didn't put up much of a fight.

That's how it went for much of the time. It was never easy but it was certainly easier than it could have been. Felicia never once asked

Jenkins if he wanted to come home, refusing to give him an out. He, however, never asked, either. Instead he accepted the Britts' authority and yet never saw his parents' decision as anything but one made out of pure love.

"I have no words for what they've done for me," Jenkins said. "None."

The bond between Jenkins and Nate developed easily.

Both wildly competitive, they tried to beat each other in everything—who would get to the car first, who would reach the top of the stairs the fastest. Some household items fell victim to their antics and the boys would try to cover their tracks. They rarely succeeded. On more than one occasion, Britt Sr. returned from a late-night shift to find things not in their proper place and the entire family enjoyed a pre-dawn wake-up call to determine the culprit.

But for the most part, the boys were low maintenance, doing most of their battles on the basketball court, and keeping the competition at a healthy level.

"There's no one I want to beat more than him," Jenkins said. "When we compete, we compete to the highest level in anything we do. Things always get heated but we were mature enough and respected each other enough that we never had to be separated or anything like that."

Apart, the competitive spirit drove the two boys. Together, it made for a lethal combination. After junior high, Jenkins and Nate enrolled at Gonzaga College High School. As sophomores, the two helped Gonzaga to a 22–6 record. At one point, the team won 15 of 17 games. Nate that year earned Gatorade player of the year honors for Washington, D.C., rising to No. 15 in his class in the national recruiting rankings.

What separated the boys from the competition? The same skills Felicia had pushed years earlier—hard work and a strong shot. Britt Sr. believed in the same mantra and when Jenkins moved in, he essentially picked up where Felicia left off. Each New Year's Day, for example, he'd bring his summer-league team to the gym at 6:00 AM and tell them to look around. No one else, he told them, was in the gym at that hour, and when June bled into July, this sort of work would be what separated them from the competition.

Pushed by their parents, the two turned into a perfect workout pair. Nate, a natural point guard and playmaker, served as the perfect setup man for the sweet-stroking Jenkins.

With two high-caliber players living under one roof, the Britt home soon became a popular spot for college coaches on the recruiting trail. Each boy enjoyed a long list of suitors—North Carolina, Arizona, Maryland, Duke, Villanova, and Virginia for Nate; Xavier, Rutgers, Miami, Clemson, and Villanova for Jenkins.

Nate was considered a more proven product, a lefty point guard who had a reputation for heady play and smart decisions. As for Jenkins, an ESPN recruiter tabbed him as a "Charles Barkley type," which is a polite way to say beefy.

"I was a fat kid," Jenkins said with a chuckle.

He was 6-foot-6 but pushing 280 pounds, and though coaches who came to visit Nate also were intrigued by Jenkins, they were concerned about his size.

"We're saying the only negative thing about this kid is he's overweight," said Jay Wright, who recruited Nate and also considered Jenkins.

With fewer issues or questions to answer, Nate was able to make his decision quickly, signing with North Carolina just as his junior year of high school began.

It wasn't so easy for Jenkins. He continued to shine on the court—as a junior, he averaged 19.8 points and 10.6 rebounds per game. He even kept the Gatorade hardware in the family, earning District of Columbia player of the year honors.

But his recruitment dragged on as the questions about his weight lingered.

When Wright brought Jenkins on campus for a visit, he sat him down for a dose of honesty that he figured would scare Jenkins away. Wright told him that if he wanted to play for Villanova, he'd have to change his diet and lifestyle significantly, cut his body fat, and make sacrifices that would be both difficult and never ending. And then the bottom line—if he didn't commit to such a program, he couldn't play for Wright.

"We just said that was reality," Wright said. "And he became very interested in us. Once we saw that he wanted that, we said, 'We got something special here.'"

In August 2013, just before his senior year was to begin, Jenkins committed to Villanova.

That same year, Felicia took an assistant's job at a Division I school—only it was at Jackson State University, in Jackson, Mississippi. Britt Sr. noticed that his mother's distance was wearing on Jenkins, so he flew him to Mississippi for a visit. There, the two had a heart-to-heart unlike any they'd had before. Jenkins confided that, while he didn't regret the move with the Britts, a part of him wondered if it was really necessary.

Felicia let her son vent and then explained why she begged to differ. She detailed the changes she'd seen in her son and the good life he'd been able to carve out for himself. Even more, she insisted that he would be neither the basketball player nor the man he is today without the dramatic intervention.

"If I could do it all over again, my choices would be the same," she said. "I do not regret it for one minute. I am forever indebted to the Britts. I tell them thank you all of the time. I know I don't have to say it but as a person and a mom, I need to say it. I have to say thank you as many times as I can."

Jenkins went home mollified, returning to Gonzaga for his senior year even as Nate transferred to Oak Hill Academy. A matchup nightmare at the high school level, Jenkins starred as a senior, winning Gatorade area player of the year honors for the second consecutive year.

In the summer after graduation, he headed to Villanova. He took a few classes, worked out with his teammates, and for the first time met John Shackleton, the Wildcats' strength and conditioning coach. A straight talker from just outside of Philadelphia, Shackleton is a former high school linebacker turned marathon runner. He works solely for the Villanova men's and women's basketball teams, designing their workouts and strength training regimens, as well as monitoring their nutrition.

He weighs and measures the body fat of each incoming freshman, beginning a chart he'll plot for the length of their college career. When Shackleton first met Jenkins he was completely stymied. Jenkins weighed in at 278 pounds, with 24 percent body fat. Shackleton weighed his numbers. Jenkins was considered obese.

Shackleton had seen a few athletes—mostly football players, particularly offensive linemen—measure similarly but never a basketball player.

"I was like, how is this dude playing basketball at this level?" Shackleton said. "How is he getting up the floor? And how is he ever going to play for us?"

Wright had the same question. He asked Shackleton for reasonable expectations for Jenkins at summer's end and by October, when the real preseason began. Shackleton, confronted with an athlete he'd never encountered, didn't want to make a promise he couldn't keep. He knew Jenkins would drop weight quickly but he simply told his coach that he'd see results.

And then he set out to make them happen, essentially remaking Jenkins' entire lifestyle.

Out went the sugars, the juices, and all processed foods. In came the vegetables and protein. Shackleton explained that Jenkins could have an omelet for breakfast, even with cheese, but no more hash browns or tater tots on the side. For lunch he steered him toward grilled chicken, rice, and vegetables, and for dinner, suggested salmon. Yes, Jenkins could have his beloved Chipotle but he'd have to choose his fillings and toppings wisely, and limit his number of visits during the week.

Every Monday and Friday, before and after the weekend, Jenkins would come by for a weigh in.

"It's a constant education," Shackleton said. "I'm always texting him, especially on the weekends."

When he wasn't directing Jenkins' diet, Shackleton was designing workouts. He wanted to keep Jenkins' body on its toes, so he changed the plan almost daily, from aerobic work to circuit training to running on an underwater treadmill to hot yoga. Shackleton viewed Jenkins' training as a challenge; Jenkins saw it more as a necessary evil.

"So when I got here, I had a little chip on my shoulder," Jenkins said. "I felt like I had to prove I could play at this level."

Motivated by that chip, Jenkins did the seemingly impossible. Instead of gaining the freshman 15 at college, he steadily lost weight. When his friends, and even his teammates, ordered takeout in the dormitories, he took a pass. He wasn't perfect. Wright recalled following

Jenkins into a store after the team had finished a dinner on the road. Without Jenkins realizing, the coach watched his player go to the checkout counter to purchase candy bars and juice.

"I said, 'Oh no,'" Wright said. "And I made him put it back."

But Shackleton didn't expect Jenkins to be perfect, knowing that to suggest he never cheat would only be setting Jenkins up to fail. Instead, Shackleton told him to aim for making the right choice 80 percent of the time.

"I told him, 'I'm not here to blast you. If you eat French fries, just tell me,'" Shackleton said.

More often than not, Jenkins hit his mark. The weight steadily came off, each weigh-in showing Jenkins' progress.

Though the pounds dropped easily, conditioning took more time. Wright loved Jenkins' game, especially his fearlessness and confidence in his shot, but after too many minutes Jenkins would get too tired to play with the energy Villanova's hard-scrabble style demands. The coach would have no choice but to sub Jenkins out.

Like every athlete, Jenkins was itching to play. He'd call his mother sometimes, disappointed that his floor time was limited—he averaged just 11 minutes per game in his freshman season—but Felicia, always a coach, told him to just keep working. Instead of calling Wright to complain about her son's minutes, she'd call the coach and tell him to just keep doing what he was doing.

"I told Coach Jay that whatever you give my son, you make sure he earns it," Felicia said. "The struggle was real there for a while. Who in college wants to go out and get a plain salad with a little dressing? But he put in the work."

Jenkins tasted a little reward in his sophomore season, upping his minutes to 18 per game, but it wasn't until his junior year that he really became a steady contributor for the Wildcats.

DANA O'NEIL

In today's college basketball culture, a three-year wait to earn significant playing time is an eternity. Most players—from the top recruits to the middling ones—dream of being a "one and done," serving the bare minimum college requirements before jumping into the professional NBA ranks.

For Jenkins to not only put in all of that work but wait for his chance showed remarkable patience and maturity.

"Everybody has their own path," Jenkins said simply. "You can't worry about anyone else's."

Jenkins stayed his own course. He began his junior season weighing just 235 pounds, his body fat down to 10 percent. "I have before and after pictures," Shackleton said. "And they're unreal."

The last step—his conditioning—and the team's needs ultimately converged at the perfect place. In 2014–15, Darrun Hilliard not only led the Wildcats in scoring, he served as the team's most reliable long-distance shooting threat. But Hilliard had graduated, leaving an opening for a great shooter.

Enter Jenkins. Even in his limited minutes in the years prior, he'd shown he wasn't shy. As both a freshman and a sophomore he launched more three-point attempts than two-point shots. Brazen and confident, it was as if Jenkins was born to play for Wright. The coach has a favorite saying when it comes to his offensive philosophy—"shoot 'em up or live in the streets." Roughly translated it means you can't make 'em if you don't take 'em.

It's a clever saying based on a slightly more scientific analysis. A few years earlier, after a conscious decision to recruit better shooters such as Jenkins, Wright turned to Billy Lange, his former assistant and an analytics savant to see how to best utilize his players. Lange studied the question in detail, handing over a 37-page report that included pie charts and graphs. Lange determined that a team doesn't win by making

Jay Wright became the head coach at Villanova, the program he grew up rooting for in the Philadelphia suburbs, in 2001, after almost taking the same position at Rutgers. (Newscom)

Top: Soon after arriving on campus, Wright began recruiting highly rated players such as Randy Foye (left) and Kyle Lowry. In the NCAA Tournament, the Wildcats reached the Sweet 16 in 2004–05, the Elite Eight in 2005–06, and the Final Four in 2008–09.

Right: Father Rob Hagan, an associate athletic director and a regular on the Villanova bench, maintains an open-door policy when it comes to the players. (USA Today Sports Images)

The son of two Villanova graduates, Ryan Arcidiacono dreamed of being a Wildcat as a kid and joined the program in 2012.

After returning to the U.S. from Nigeria, Daniel Ochefu became the "one" in Wright's four-out, one-in offensive system.

Kris Jenkins (left) left home and moved in with the family of Nate Britt in 2006. Improbably, the two brothers would meet in the national championship game 10 years later.

(USA Today Sports Images)

Josh Hart led the 2015–16 Wildcats in scoring at 15.5 points per game.

Despite stability on the coaching staff and the presence of many talented players, the Wildcats failed to make deep runs in the NCAA Tournament after their Final Four season in 2008–09. They were upset in the second round by Saint Mary's in 2009–10 (top) and by N.C. State in 2014–15 (bottom). (USA Today Sports Images/Newscom)

With Ochefu sprawled on the court behind him, Marcus Paige's double-pump three-pointer with 4.7 seconds left in the national championship game between North Carolina and Villanova seemed to send the contest into overtime, until...

Bang.

Tens of thousands gathered outside City Hall in Philadelphia to celebrate Villanova's national championship (top), where Arcidiacono posed with the championship trophy (middle) and Wright and Philadelphia mayor Jim Kenney flashed the V-sign alongside Villanova president Father Peter Donahue (bottom).

the highest percentage of three-pointers but by taking and making the most shots overall.

It's essentially basic math.

"If we look at it and say they had shot 28 percent from three, but say they made eight and we only made three, they're going to beat you," Wright said. "It's not that complicated."

Armed with that information, not to mention enough confidence to let his team play with some freedom, Wright gave his players the green light to shoot. It is not an anything-goes philosophy. Wright expects his players to take smart shots and to be discerning, but he is more willing than many coaches to live with the occasional mistake. He believes in Lange's data but even more he believes that an athlete is more confident if he's not looking over his shoulder, worried that he'll be yanked for every poor decision.

Jenkins is the personification of shoot 'em up or live in the streets, both good and bad.

"Oh, I've slept in the streets," he said.

Where other players might be less aggressive if their shots stop falling, Jenkins doesn't blink. He keeps firing. Some of that, certainly, is innate. Some people are born with the gift of letting mistakes roll off their backs more easily than others. Jenkins has some of that. That Big Smoove nickname fit his chill personality as much as his game style.

But Jenkins also was gifted with confidence at a young age. Though she may have been boring her son with the monotony of those old-school shots, Jenkins' mother also was instilling that confidence.

"I believe every shot is going in, no matter how I catch it, no matter where I catch it," Jenkins said. "I've always been that way. The belief and the confidence my mom gave me. When she was teaching me, she always told me that if you believe it's going in, then it has a better chance of going in. That's anything in life. If you believe it, you can do it."

Britt Sr. essentially delivered the same message when Jenkins came into his life.

"What people saw him do at Villanova, that's the same thing we've been preaching to him," Britt Sr. said. "Kris has played in so many tough games, against high-level teams, even teams with guys older than him. He would miss and then he'd hit a winning shot. He believed in what we were doing because we believed in him."

And now Wright breeds the same sort of conviction in his players.

The only difference in college is that there is a price. In exchange for offensive freedom, Wright asks his players for an unwavering commitment to defense. He expects his players to be relentless as they challenge their opponents. They can take liberties and risks on offense. They cannot do the same on defense.

For years, it was an exchange Jenkins' body simply wouldn't allow him to make. Still trying to build his stamina, when his energy waned Jenkins became too much of a liability on defense. In his junior season, he could finally hold up at both ends of the court. Jenkins averaged 28 minutes per game; only Arcidiacono and Hart put in more time.

And as the season progressed, each game becoming more critical, Jenkins' playing time increased. In the final month of the regular season, he spent 30 minutes per game on the court, numbers his old body never would have been able to maintain.

"He put in the work. He made the sacrifices," Shackleton said.

In the NCAA Tournament, Jenkins was nearly indispensable. He played 31 minutes in the second-round game against Iowa, 35 in the Wildcats' Sweet 16 matchup against Miami, 28 against Kansas in the Elite Eight, and 32 in the national semifinal against Oklahoma.

But against North Carolina, foul trouble turned Jenkins into a spectator for much of the game. He was whistled for his second infraction less than five minutes into the first half and Wright had no choice but to pull him. Jenkins re-entered with 6:33 left until halftime. In a taut battle between the Tar Heels and the Wildcats, Villanova's best shooter would play just eight first-half minutes, scoring only six points.

Living the lesson of attitude that Wright had preached, though, Jenkins tried to impact the game from the bench.

"No head down, positive, cheering on my teammates," he said. "I knew I'd have to go in for offense/defense at some point, so I was just always encouraging, willing to cheer on the next man because that's my brother."

But the time on the bench cost Jenkins his rhythm. He missed his first four shots to start the second half, and robbed of its most reliable shooter, Villanova fell behind 43–38. Things got worse before they got better for Jenkins. In the span of 12 seconds, beginning with 7:02 left in the game, Jenkins was whistled for his third and fourth fouls. He left the game with 6:50 left and did not return until there was 2:44 remaining and Villanova, which once had led by as many as 10, up by only five.

For the remainder of the game, Wright would swap Jenkins in and out of the game, bringing him on the floor when the Wildcats were on offense, yanking him out when they were playing defense to protect him from drawing his fifth and final foul.

Except Jenkins could never quite find his stroke. Good shooters typically get into a groove, relying on rhythm and adrenaline as much as technique. Time on the bench, rotating in and out of the lineup, can rob even the most confident shooter of his touch. Jenkins certainly felt that.

Twenty seconds after he came back into the game and with Villanova holding just a five-point lead, the 85 percent free-throw shooter clanked the first shot of a one-and-one attempt.

"I had never seen him do that in three years," Arcidiacono said. "He's such a good shooter and for him to miss is so uncharacteristic. I said to him, 'Hey, don't get nervous on me now, bro,' and he just looked at me and said, 'I got you.'"

In those last minutes, Jenkins would revolve in and out of the game twice more. Wright finally sent his top shooter to the court for good with exactly one minute to play and Villanova up by just one point.

All of that, then, makes Jenkins' hero shot all the more remarkable. Before he launched the final shot of the 2015–16 season, Jenkins went seven minutes and 50 seconds without a point, more than two minutes without so much as flicking his wrists and taking a shot. That's an eternity.

Yet when asked what amazed him most about the last play, Jenkins didn't cite his nerve in taking the shot or even the improbability of making it.

"I never get that shot in practice," Jenkins said. "Never."

The Wildcats run through Nova at every practice, the defense presented dictating exactly how the play will unfold. The ball never ends up in Jenkins' hands. That's partially because the Villanova players serving as defenders know the play so well. They're familiar with every possible pass and twist. Plus, they know just how good a shooter Jenkins is. Given all of the offensive options to consider on the court, they simply aren't going to allow Jenkins to be one of them.

North Carolina was certainly familiar with Jenkins. In the NCAA Tournament alone, he had shot 27-of-47 from the floor, good for 57 percent. Plus, technology and televised games means there are no surprises. Surely Carolina was familiar with the Wildcats' endgame play. Villanova ran a variation of Nova in 2009, with Scottie Reynolds driving the length of the floor against Pittsburgh in a regional final. Just weeks earlier, in the Big East Tournament final, Arcidiacono was left with the same last-second choice against Seton Hall, only he opted to shoot. He missed and the Pirates won the league tournament.

But seeing something and defending it are two different animals. Fearing a Hail Mary, length-of-the-court heave, Brice Johnson, who would have been guarding Jenkins as he inbounded the ball, dropped all the way back and under the opposite basket. Jenkins was essentially unguarded underneath the North Carolina basket.

Basketball historians would argue that was Roy Williams' first mistake. In the unforgettable 1992 regional final in Philadelphia, then Kentucky coach Rick Pitino left Grant Hill unguarded as he inbounded the ball for Duke. Hill fired a perfect 70-foot pass to Christian Laettner, who caught the ball, turned, and sunk a game winner to send Duke to the Final Four.

Pitino later conceded he had made a tactical error.

Williams, though, thought he had made the right call 24 years later.

"They had to take it about 75 feet before they got to the basket," he said after the game.

But Duke and Laettner only had 2.1 seconds to pull off a miracle. Villanova had 4.7 seconds, plenty of time to cover the distance. And as soon as Jenkins bounced the ball in to Arcidiacono, he was essentially unguarded and wide open for the duration of the play.

"I knew if I could get anywhere near Ryan, I'd be wide open," Jenkins said.

Recognizing that, Jenkins trailed his senior teammate the entire length of the court. He took 10 full steps at almost a jog pace, purposefully hanging back behind Arcidiacono.

As he neared midcourt, Jenkins raised his hands and turned toward Arcidiacono.

"I couldn't believe how wide open I was," Jenkins said.

Neither could Williams. Though he wanted the home-run pass covered, he didn't intend to concede so much real estate to a shooter who has the sort of range that Jenkins has.

"I wanted him more covered," a despondent Williams said after the title game. "I hoped we'd get up to him closer."

Instead, Jenkins, accelerated his pace and started shuffling his feet, making sure that when he caught the ball he'd be in stride for a fluid release on his shot.

By then Britt Sr. had swapped sides. With her two boys facing each other in the biggest game of the year, an emotional Melody, paced the concourse but Britt Sr. split his allegiances. He sat among the Villanova fans, wearing his Villanova gear for the first half. At halftime, he ducked into a restroom, swapped his T-shirt for a North Carolina version, and sat among the Tar Heel faithful.

Britt Sr. was sitting next to his brother, a North Carolina law school graduate, during the final timeout. He watched Villanova set up the play, saw the Tar Heels' defensive alignment, and quietly nudged his brother.

"I saw they didn't have anybody on the inbounds man—on Kris—and I said, 'If he catches it, it's over,'" Britt Sr. said. "My brother said, 'Man, who you rooting for?' I said, 'I'm just telling you.'"

Since the two met, Britt Sr. told Jenkins his bread and butter would be his shot. Jenkins, he figured, would max out his height and be a tweener in terms of position—big for a guard, but small for a forward. Knowing Jenkins couldn't make himself grow, Britt Sr. encouraged Jenkins to work on that which he could control.

"I told him to work on your footwork. It's always about your footwork," Britt Sr. said.

Which is how Britt Sr. and Felicia Jenkins, separated by the entire width of the court in the national championship game, came to be staring at the exact same place—at Jenkins' feet. The two coaches who knew their boy so well didn't even need to watch his follow-through. Just as Felicia saw how set Jenkins' feet were set, Britt Sr. watched Jenkins time his stride just right, slowing his speed so he was essentially tiptoeing as Arcidiacono readied to flip him the ball.

His footwork spot on, Jenkins was able to catch, plant, and rise up for the shot in one fluid motion.

Quickly realizing their mistake, the Tar Heels tried to regroup. By the time Isaiah Hicks flashed out toward Jenkins, Jenkins already was flicking the ball off of his fingertips and toward the rim.

As the ball arced toward the basket, Jenkins bent over at the waist and followed it, waiting to see if it would slip through the net or bounce off the rim.

In the stands, Felicia mimicked her son's posture, putting her hands on her knees, almost as if she were in a defensive stance. She can't remember breathing but she does remember her mind quickly retracing the path she and Jenkins took to get to that moment—all of the heartaches and difficult decisions, Kori's passing and Jenkins' moving, all the way back to those early days on the basketball court, practicing boring old jumpers.

"It felt like the longest time," she said. "That ball was in the air forever."

Flicked from Kris Jenkins' fingertips, the ball tracked toward the net. Where it landed would determine more than just the 2016 national champion. If it slipped through the net, it would vindicate and validate. If it missed—wide right, wide left, long, or short—it could lead to the latest in a series of excruciating NCAA Tournament losses for Villanova.

Or so went the collective thinking, that this basketball team would be defined by which direction that basketball went.

Hours earlier, in the quiet of the locker room, Father Rob Hagan stood before the Villanova players for the final pregame prayer and message of the season. The priest and associate athletic director likes to find a hook for his young players, a way to connect a deeper purpose to a simple basketball game. In previous weeks he'd connected his Gospel message to Rocky Balboa and the 1980 U.S. Olympic gold medal ice hockey team, both upstart champions. Villanova, he'd told them, knows all about being underdogs. It's part of the team's identity, dating all the way back to 1985 when the eighth-seeded Wildcats upset Georgetown for their first national title.

In the minutes before Villanova tipped off against North Carolina, hours before Jenkins would launch that fateful shot, Hagan looked at the players surrounding him and delivered a simple, yet powerful, message.

"Tonight, I don't really need any of those other examples," he said. "The example is you."

On face value, the 2016 Villanova basketball team as an underdog would seem a hard sell. For three weeks, the Wildcats held the No. 1 ranking in the nation and rolled into the NCAA Tournament as a No. 2 seed, courtesy of their 29–5 record. But underdogs aren't merely borne out of statistics; perceptions mold them, too, and no matter how many games it won, no matter how high its ranking soared, Villanova couldn't quiet the skeptics.

Before the season, Las Vegas odds makers made Villanova a 25-1 shot to win the national title, giving the Wildcats the same chance as Wichita State, Gonzaga, Michigan, Arizona, and UConn. Before the NCAA Tournament, the odds improved only marginally, to 12–1. Prior to the actual championship game, even after the Wildcats dispatched of Oklahoma in the national semifinal in a record-setting thrashing, North Carolina was tabbed the 2.5-point favorite.

Hagan knew all of that, the perception at least if not the actual odds. So did everyone else in that locker room. Villanova players and coaches had spent the better part of the entire season answering questions about what they'd failed to accomplish in the past instead of what they had achieved in the present. They knew for every fan sitting in Houston's NRG Stadium there were probably two, maybe more, critics who doubted their chances and were waiting, if not flat-out expecting, them to fail.

But played correctly, there's also something liberating about being an underdog. No one expects much of them. They aren't supposed to win. So while everyone else spent the entirety of the NCAA Tournament putting pressure on Villanova to win, listing their past failures as proof of what they wouldn't accomplish in the present, the Wildcats stopped worrying.

As that ball hung in the air and the game in the balance, as everyone else waited to measure Villanova's season on how the ball bounced, the Wildcats long ago had agreed they wouldn't let the last game, no matter when it occurred, define them.

"This team," Jay Wright said, "had no fear of failing."

Perhaps the reason Villanova had no fear of failure was because it had failed so much before. In the 10 years from 2006 through 2015, the Wildcats strung together a record of 243–98 and earned nine NCAA Tournament bids. They appeared in a Final Four, two Elite Eights, and three Sweet 16s.

But sports exist in a what-have-you-done-for-me-lately vacuum, and college basketball is even more unforgiving, asking what have you done for me in March? Forget using logic to explain away the illogic of the NCAA Tournament, of a single-elimination tournament in which one bad night—or even one bad second or shot—can negate the value of four-plus months' work. Fair or unfair, sane or insane, if a college basketball team wins from November through February but loses in March, its season is automatically devalued. That's reality.

And despite those glitzy numbers and what, by any other measure, would add up to a stirring success, by basketball math Villanova was failing. That's because, after reaching the Final Four in 2009, the Wildcats hadn't gotten out of the NCAA Tournament's first weekend. Five bids in six years and not a single Sweet 16 to show for it:

In 2010, Villanova finished the regular season 24–7 and earned a No. 2 seed. The Wildcats lost to 10th-seeded Saint Mary's in the second round.

In 2011, Villanova finished the regular season 21–11 and earned a No. 9 seed. The Wildcats lost to mid-major George Mason in the first round.

In 2013, Villanova finished the regular season 20–13 and earned a No. 9 seed. The Wildcats lost to eighth-seeded North Carolina in the first round.

In 2014, Villanova finished the regular season 28–4 and earned a No. 2 seed. The Wildcats lost to seventh-seeded Connecticut in the second round.

In 2015, Villanova finished the regular season 32–2 and earned a No. 1 seed. The Wildcats lost to eighth-seeded North Carolina State in the second round.

Individually each season was disappointing, an abrupt finish to what figured to be a long NCAA run. Collectively the five early exits branded the Wildcats as an underachiever and worse, a team of smoke and mirrors that wasn't cut out for the rigors of March.

"It upset me," Daniel Ochefu said. "We didn't want to be known as the team that's always highly ranked but gets knocked out early."

Each end brought its own share of misery but the worst, no doubt, came in 2015. That year, the 30th anniversary of the Wildcats' 1985 national championship, set up as a perfect celebratory season. With two seniors, JayVaughn Pinkston and Darrun Hilliard, who had endured a 13–19 season as freshmen and shepherded Villanova back to national prominence, the Wildcats had a roster stacked with talent and experience.

They lived up to it, too, opening the season with 13 wins in a row and climbing up to the No. 6 spot in the national polls. The Wildcats would, in fact, lose just two games in the entire regular season—to Seton Hall in overtime and to Georgetown—push their ranking to fourth in the nation, win a school-record 32 games as well as the Big East regular-season crown and, for the first time in 20 years, the Big East Tournament title.

In the last four games before the NCAA Tournament, Villanova topped opponents by an average of 25 points per game, and when the NCAA Tournament Selection Committee convened, the members considered the Wildcats' body of work and awarded them a No. 1 seed, ranking them behind only Kentucky in the field of 68.

Not everyone agreed with the seeding. Though Villanova had played six ranked opponents during the course of the season, three of them—Michigan, VCU, and St. John's—would skid out of the top 25 midway through the year and only two, No. 22 Butler and No. 23 Georgetown, retained their rankings heading into the NCAA Tournament.

"The Villanova Wildcats are wonderful," respected sportswriter Mike DeCourcy wrote in *The Sporting News*. "They are everything one could want a college basketball team to be: together, consistent, tenacious, skilled, smart. All the good stuff. But they aren't as talented as the other teams considered for the No. 1 seed spots. And they are less accomplished than most. They are the kings of 'very good.' They aren't the second-best team, and they haven't had the second-best season."

Certainly the Wildcats were aware of the criticism as they headed to Pittsburgh for the first weekend of the NCAA Tournament. They knew it was as much a byproduct of their recent history as their most recent season.

They also knew that, despite beating Lafayette by 41 points in the first round, not everyone was sold on Villanova.

"We know that we are judged on getting to the second weekend," Jay Wright said in the postgame press conference after beating Lafayette. "You know once you get to that second weekend everyone is pleased with you. If you don't, you know everyone's going to question you."

The coach, then, wasn't surprised when the questions began two nights later after N.C. State sent Villanova packing, 71–68. The Wildcats played terribly, allowing the Wolfpack guards to slice their defense with ease, and shot just 9-of-28 from the three-point line to become the first No. 1 seed ousted from the tournament field. The loss, in fact, was so bad it inspired an Internet sensation, a meme of a piccolo player from the school's pep band, tears streaming as she played her instrument.

In the locker room, long after reporters were allowed into the room, the players sat and stared vacantly, too stunned to even explain what happened. Ochefu recalled the scene vividly. He'd experienced some variation of the same March postgame atmosphere in each of his three seasons at Villanova. Seeing Pinkston and Hiliard hit him especially hard.

"I remember all three years but that was the worst," he said. "It was bad. We wanted so badly to see them go out on top."

Later, Wright would wonder if that was part of the problem. Maybe his players wanted it so much they had become consumed by it, turning that second-round game into something much bigger than it should have been. Perhaps, he thought, they had started to believe what they were hearing, that their failures in March negated everything else they had accomplished. That had never been the coach's message but maybe what he'd been preaching—that one game couldn't define a team, that a postseason loss doesn't erase months of regular-season excellence—was falling on deaf ears.

"Maybe we thought too much about proving ourselves rather than just thinking about ourselves," Wright conceded.

Wright knew personally how easy it was to confuse the two. Years earlier he rode triumphantly onto the suburban Philadelphia campus to save the day. Hot off a successful run at Hofstra, he had become *the* top young coach in the country and now he was at Villanova, the favorite team of his childhood, ready to restore the program's glory. He immediately landed one of the most heralded recruiting classes in the country, sounding the gong that happy days indeed were coming to the school again.

But as the young Wildcats went through their growing pains, finding their way as college players and learning to play for Wright, the team went three years without an NCAA bid, a gross under-achievement for a rabid fan base desperate for instant success. People questioned Wright's coaching acumen and wondered if perhaps he was in over his head. One fan told a local newspaper reporter that Wright was little more than an empty suit and deserved to be fired.

Rare is the coach who doesn't go through such turmoil. Before he became arguably the greatest coach of all time, Mike Krzyzewski went 38–47 in his first three seasons at Duke. Unimpressed by the young coach from Army with the hard-to-pronounce surname, more than a few boosters called then athletic director Tom Butters demanding he fire the coach. Butters refused and the rest, as they say, is history.

Villanova administrators similarly stood their ground when the grumbling around Wright began. They told their coach they trusted his vision, and never so much as suggested he win fast. But young coaches aren't unlike young players. Though they're told to ignore the outside criticism, it's easy to get caught up in it.

Told at one point that, with fans at least, he was on the hot seat, the coach laughed.

"I deserve to be," he said.

But that season, rather than being consumed by what outsiders wanted him to do, Wright took a hard look at what he was doing. He asked his staff for honest assessments and made a few of his own, and, though perhaps it wasn't what people wanted to hear, he determined that his team was progressing. It was incremental, slower certainly than fans would have liked—slower, frankly, than he would have preferred—but it was there. The postseason, he decided, wasn't a fair evaluator of his team's development, and though he acknowledged and even respected what the fan base was craving, he refused to pander to it.

"It was clear as day for the media, the fans, and some of the alumni that the case was maybe this guy had to go but I was okay with that," Wright said. "But I knew we were good. They were getting better."

That following season, in 2004–05, Villanova—and Wright— would have its breakthrough year, winning 24 games and reaching the Sweet 16.

That's the same lesson, Wright realized, he had to impart to his team following the 2015 season. They needed to own the losses, to understand and appreciate why their fans were disappointed. They could even be disappointed themselves. The loss certainly pained Wright. He didn't watch film from the N.C. State game for a full two months, and even then only turned on the laptop when he was alone, flying across the country.

But he didn't want them to be so preoccupied with March that they ignored everything else.

"We had to tell these guys that we're going to enjoy a basketball season," Wright said. "The players only get so many years to play. We wanted them to understand, don't dismiss this season because you have to get past the first round. Enjoy this season."

The players wanted to believe it. What Wright said made sense but it was also difficult to dismiss what they'd seen in the years prior. For three years, the seniors had watched as graduating players sobbed their way out of the locker room. Now it was their turn. How could they finish any differently?

"I remember after we lost in the tournament Coach said that this team coming back has a chance to be special," Ochefu said. "But I was probably the biggest doubter that we could be better than we were."

But Wright was as relentless in hammering home that message as he was demanding effort. He reaffirmed it daily, saying it with such conviction that ultimately players believed it. Of course, in the cocoon of team-only exercises it was easy. Outside the bubble it was a different story.

Before Villanova so much as held an organized practice, people were asking how the players would get past the postseason hurdle, insisting that nothing outside of the NCAA Tournament mattered for this team. In October, at the annual Big East media day gathering at Madison Square Garden, Villanova was picked as the favorite to win the league. Rather than field questions about their role as the top dog, they answered questions about their hangdog losses.

Just as he told his team to do, Wright owned it. Neither he nor his players—Ochefu and Ryan Arcidiacono attended the event—tried to downplay the impact of those losses. They didn't apologize but they also didn't try to argue.

"There's no way to combat it," Wright said that day. "That's why I say we have to own it. That's the mystical thing about college basketball. It doesn't matter how many games you win or lose. You're judged on March. There's nothing we can do about that label. It's going to be that way all year. We can't get past it until we get there, and then when we get there, we have to win to get past it."

As Wright predicted, the skepticism chased Villanova all season and when the Wildcats lost early—and badly—to Oklahoma and Virginia, their only ranked opponents in the first two months of the season, it exploded. Once ranked as high as eighth in the nation, Villanova plummeted to No. 17 after the loss to the Cavaliers. Even as they regrouped, winning their next nine in a row and slowly climbing back up the polls to as high as No. 4, they were dogged by critics. The Big East was not the Big Ten or the ACC, and though Villanova beat two ranked opponents in that run—pummeling No. 6 Xavier by 31 points and winning at No. 18 Butler—the team struggled to earn the same sort of uniform respect as others in the top 25.

On February 8, 2016, Villanova earned its first No. 1 ranking in program history, taking the top spot in the polls courtesy of its own 20–3 record and perhaps even more, losses by Oklahoma and North Carolina, the previous week's Nos. 1 and 2 teams, respectively.

And yet…

"After two straight incredible regular seasons and two spectacular tournament flameouts, the college basketball world has two words for Villanova: prove it," one national website opined, voicing the opinion of plenty. With each passing game it was as if Villanova was on a collision course with March, and the closer the pivotal month came, the more the conversation tunneled in on the Wildcats' past losses.

"Even other coaches, they'd try to be nice and say, 'Hey, congrats on being ranked No. 1,'" Wright said. "But then they'd say, 'Hey, but the only thing that matters for you guys is the NCAA Tournament.'"

Philadelphia is a city accustomed to sporting disappointment. Residents wear their cynicism like a badge of honor and practically steel themselves against letdown. The Philadelphia Phillies' World Series title in 2008 ended a 23-year title drought for the city, two-plus decades not just marked by futility, but even more cruelly, agonizingly close near misses. The Flyers have made the Stanley Cup Finals eight times in their history and as recently as 2010; they haven't hoisted the Cup since 1975. The Eagles have made it to the NFC Championship Game six times, including a run of four consecutive appearances from 2001 to 2005; they have yet to win a Super Bowl. As for the 76ers, despite a rich tradition including Julius Erving, Charles Barkley, and Allen Iverson, they haven't reached an NBA Final since 2001 and more recently have been one of the worst franchises in the NBA. Even locally bred horse Smarty Jones came up just short. The thoroughbred won the Kentucky Derby and the Preakness in 2004 but lost the Belmont Stakes—and the Triple Crown—by a head to long shot Birdstone.

Villanova, constantly teasing locals with a great regular season only to lose when it mattered most, merely added to Philadelphia's misery.

But by March 2016, with the 76ers already eliminated from anything but a good spot in the draft lottery, the Flyers barely squeaking into the playoffs, the Phillies projected to lose more than they'd win, and the Eagles just months removed from firing head coach Chip Kelly, the Wildcats were the talk of the town.

"It's been a tough time for Philly," said Arcidiacono, who grew up outside the city. "But we can't take on that burden."

On March 13 the Wildcats were awarded a No. 2 seed, slated to play UNC Asheville in the first round on Friday, March 18, in Brooklyn. By now Villanova was hardly in awe of the circus atmosphere. The players knew the routine; they'd practice privately as well as hold a pseudo-practice for fans at the Barclay Center on Thursday, and they'd answer questions at a press conference and in the locker rooms.

And by now, the Wildcats knew what the questions would be. Seated on the dais, Wright, Arcidiacono, Ochefu, Josh Hart, and Kris Jenkins were asked 22 questions in all. Eight of them were couched in one way or another to address the previous years' losses.

No one can pinpoint when Wright's message of valuing the season and not worrying about the postseason became believable. Maybe there wasn't a moment. Maybe it was more a slow burn building as the players grew sick of hearing it, or, one by one realized there was nothing they could do to change it. But at some point their angst at being labeled a failure, their worry about not fulfilling their own dreams, disappeared.

Instead of feeling the pressures from losing or bearing the burdens of expectations, the Wildcats decided to adopt the underdog mentality. What, they asked, did they have to lose?

"We're not afraid to lose. We've been there before. We've lost early and had everyone hate on us, so how much worse can it get?" Arcidiacono said in the days before that first NCAA game. "We came through it so what's to be afraid of? It happens. We've lost. We've been inconsistent. We've had all of that happen to us already, so why be afraid?"

There is a difference, any coach will tell you, between playing to win and playing not to lose. Teams stuck in the latter mindset look anxious and play tight, as if every shot is the biggest one of their careers. They make mistakes because they try too hard rather than simply play the game. That's essentially how Villanova played in 2015 against N.C. State and that's actually how the Wildcats looked early against UNC Asheville. The Bulldogs' tricky 1-3-1 zone kept things interesting in the first half, keeping the usually good shooting Wildcats on their heels.

With just a little more than four minutes left until the break, Villanova led by just two.

One play changed the entire tenor of the game, if not the Wildcats' NCAA fates entirely. Arcidiacono missed a three-pointer, the 10th clank in 13 attempts for Villanova at that point. But the senior chased down his own miss and, seven seconds later, found Mikal Bridges open beyond the arc. The freshman drained the open shot, the first of four consecutive three-pointers Villanova would make in the final 2:39 of the half. The Wildcats led the stunned Bulldogs by 14 at the break and UNC Asheville would never get within single digits again, eventually losing by 30.

Arcidiacono said afterward his offensive rebound was little more than a hustle play, an aggressive move to keep Villanova's possession alive. It's hard now not to look at it in the bigger picture. It was as if that one play freed the Wildcats from their inhibitions and worries. At that moment what they said—that they didn't fear losing—became how they played. In a tournament stocked with upsets, nailbiters, and crazy finishes, the Wildcats cruised.

The same team derided for years for its inability to win at the most critical times turned the NCAA Tournament into a walkover.

Certainly it didn't hurt that Villanova was afforded a relatively easy first-weekend ride. The NCAA Tournament Selection Committee opted not to make the Wildcats the No. 2 seed in the East Region, which would have meant regional games in Philadelphia, and instead placed them in the South. But the committee did give them more winnable opening-round games. Iowa, the seventh seed and the Cats' second-round opponent, limped into the NCAA Tournament. Once ranked as high as fifth in the nation, the Hawkeyes fell apart down the stretch of the regular season. They lost five of their final seven regular-season games and were bounced out of the Big Ten Tournament by Illinois in the first round.

Still, Villanova's reversal of fortune was nothing shy of stunning. For all its struggles, Iowa remained a high-scoring team (ranked 57th in the nation) and one good enough to have finished tied for third in its league. The game was over by halftime. Villanova hung 54 points on the Hawkeyes in the first 20 minutes, an offensive clinic in which the Wildcats shot 60 percent overall and 58 percent from beyond the arc. Villanova would lead the game for all but one minute and 28 seconds, build an advantage as large as 34 points, and win 87–68.

When it was over, though, Iowa coach Fran McCaffery didn't laud the Wildcats for their offensive prowess. A Philadelphia native and longtime friend of Wright's, McCaffery instead pointed to a less obvious statistic. Villanova made 32 shots; they assisted on 23 of them.

"They share the basketball," McCaffery said. "You've got a lot of really talented guys, but you've also got a lot of guys with strong egos.

It's clear to me that Jay has those guys committed to one thing and that's playing together."

Freed of seven years' worth of questions about their first-weekend failures, the Wildcats were finally able to embrace their success. Arcidiacono admitted he felt relieved when the buzzer finally sounded and the scoreboard showed a Villanova win. At that moment, Wright also appreciated what his players had been through. He had asked them to not judge their season by the same parameters as everyone else, had listened to them say that they would play fearlessly, but until that second-round game was in the books, the coach didn't really grasp how difficult that task had been.

"I'm 54 years old and it enters the back of my mind that people are watching what's going to happen, but at 54 I can compartmentalize that," he said. "But then I realize, these poor kids. They're not 54. They're kids. But then that Iowa game, it hit me. They really didn't care. That was the best game they'd played all season at that point and that supposedly was the game where they had the most pressure. But they didn't care. We talked about how it doesn't define you and they actually did it."

So now what? For so long the focus for Villanova had been on those first two NCAA Tournament games; now that the Wildcats were through, what was the ceiling? The players themselves never really set one. Unlike many programs that admit publicly that they are eyeing a national championship, or at least a Final Four, the Wildcats never talked about their endgame. Naturally every player wants to win a national title but it was not something this team in particular had verbalized.

To do so, they knew, would have been laughable. How could a team that struggled to win two games in a row in March expect to win six? But once they moved on, once they tossed the monkey off their backs, the Wildcats realized there was no need to change their singular focus.

"When we got past the second weekend, people realized that we were actually not a fluke," Ochefu said. "We weren't going to be a disappointment but still no one talked about going to the Final Four, winning a national championship. I heard a lot of other players from other teams talking about it but we never said it. Obviously we wanted to do it, but we weren't going to put that pressure on ourselves."

But people, of course, get greedy. Their team finally able to break the hex, Villanova fans were hardly satiated by two NCAA wins. They wanted more, evidenced by the large crowd of students and well-wishers who surrounded the Wildcats' bus on March 22 as they departed for the airport and their regional games in Louisville. With two other Philly schools, Saint Joseph's and Temple, already eliminated, Villanova reigned as the city's last hope. Suddenly, the same people who were wringing their hands, worried that the Wildcats couldn't win two games, were trying to figure out just how Villanova might win a national title.

Even Vegas fell in love with Villanova, making the Wildcats a 4.5-point favorite against Miami in the regional semifinal.

Led by two senior guards, the Hurricanes were known for slicing their way to the basket to either create shots or get to the free-throw line (Miami made more free throws than its opponents had even attempted). They also had an intangible working in their favor—a bit of snarl after they were listed as the underdogs to Wichita State in their second-round game, despite being the No. 3 seed to Wichita State's No. 11 seed.

Unlike Villanova, which had spent so many years ignoring the critics, Miami used the naysayers to fuel them.

"I feel like a lot of people think we haven't done enough to prove ourselves," senior Angel Rodriguez said after beating the Shockers.

Villanova, then, would be a fertile proving ground.

Instead, the ground was far too hot for the Hurricanes.

Miami made 10 three-pointers and shot 53 percent from the floor and lost. The Hurricanes never led once in the entire game and enjoyed one brief minute of a tied ballgame, at 0–0.

In the same state where they needed a perfect game to win a national championship 31 years earlier, Villanova was nearly flawless again. The Wildcats shot 63 percent from the floor and a staggering 67 percent from the three-point line. In a bit of foreshadowing, Kris Jenkins launched a buzzer-beating three (one of five he made in the game) just before the half with his back foot on the halfcourt logo, swishing it with ease.

"I looked at Darryl [Reynolds]. We both got eye contact like, 'Wow! That's Steph [Curry] range,'" Ochefu said of his teammate's shot.

Villanova would win going away, 92–69, and leave Miami coach Jim Larranaga at a loss for words. "When they play like that, you just have to say, 'Well…'" the coach told Yahoo!Sports, not even bothering to finish the sentence, the implication of helplessness obvious.

The win put Villanova in its third Elite Eight under Wright, on the doorstep of the Final Four.

Just two weeks earlier, on Selection Sunday, Ryan Arcidiacono's father, Joe, watched as CBS unveiled the NCAA Tournament brackets. He, like a lot of people, did a little mental projecting, trying to figure out who Villanova might face as it advanced through the tourney.

When he got to the regional final, he stopped.

Kansas? Are you kidding me? Joe remembered thinking.

"They're the best," he said. "I mean, [ESPN analyst] Jay Bilas had them and Carolina as his two top teams. And I'm like, 'Well, alright, this has been a great career, Ry.'"

The top-seeded Jayhawks, Villanova's regional-final opponent, were in fact among the tournament favorites. In ESPN's Tournament Challenge, where fans fill out an online bracket, 25 percent of the 11.57 million brackets entered had Kansas as the national champion, more than any of the 68 teams in the field. By comparison, Villanova earned just 2.6 percent of the picks. Even President Barack Obama picked Kansas to win the title—and also had the Jayhawks knocking out Villanova to get there.

It was a smart pick. Playing in the Big 12 Conference, arguably the toughest league top to bottom, Kansas won both the regular-season and tournament titles and finished the year on a 14-game tear. The Jayhawks entered the NCAA Tournament as the No. 1 team in the nation and the top seed in the field, and quickly proved they deserved both. Sixteen-seed Austin Peay proved no match for KU, losing by 26, ninth-seeded UConn earned a 12-point boot, and, in a game many expected to be close, Maryland was sent packing 79–63.

Like Villanova, Kansas had terrific shooters, a solid inside game, and a lot of experience. Unlike some of the Wildcats' earlier NCAA opponents, the Jayhawks could defend. Maryland connected on only eight of its 23 three-point attempts in the second half.

That made this a something's-gotta-give game. In its first three NCAA Tournament games, the Wildcats hit 33 of their 62 three-point attempts, demoralizing opponents with their offensive prowess. But what if Kansas didn't budge off the arc? What if the Wildcats couldn't shoot? How could they win?

The funny thing about those questions—and they were plentiful before tipoff—is that shooting never was the entirety of the Wildcats' identity, at least not by the team's thinking. Sure, they had players who could connect but during the regular season, they shot a middling 34 percent from beyond the arc. They saw themselves as scrappers, not finesse players, guys who liked to rack up those Attitude points by doing the grunt work a basketball game demands.

"From day one since I got here to right now, we're still talking about the same thing—making it ugly," Ochefu said later.

This one was exactly that. A heavyweight bout, Wright called it. He meant more the stature of both programs at the time but it was an apt analogy for the game, too—two foes standing toe to toe to see which would fall first. Villanova landed the first punch, taking a seven-point lead at the half but Kansas answered with its own one-two, first regaining the lead and then stretching the advantage to five points with 10:50 to play.

The pro-Kansas crowd threatened to blow the roof off of the KFC Yum! Center rafters, but rather than call for a panicked timeout, Wright let his team play on. He trusted their instinct, and more trusted their resolve. This was really the first time in the entire tournament that Villanova was a legit underdog but he knew his team long had owned that personality.

His faith was rewarded immediately. Villanova went on a 10–0 run in classic Villanova fashion—four different players combined to score the 10 points. Though Kansas threatened, getting two last-ditch chances to tie or take the lead, Jayhawks would never lead again. Instead the Wildcats marched to the free-throw line eight times and made all eight shots to seal the 64–59 win and a spot in the Final Four.

"At that point I was thinking of where I was every single time I've worked on my free throws thoughout my life," said Arcidiacono, who hit four of them. "This one gym, just by myself with no one in the gym. I was thinking about how we always end practice shooting free throws. I thought about our video director, because we were working on my free throws throughout the whole year, and I found a groove throughout the end of the year. I was confident it was going to go in."

After the game was over, a euphoric Arcidiacono ran around the court in celebration. The senior remembered he did the same thing as a high schooler and Villanova fan in 2009 after Scottie Reynolds drove the length of the court to beat Pitt and punch a Villanova ticket to the Final Four. He never thought he'd have the chance to do it himself.

He also remembered the previous NCAA Tournament, when he purposefully ignored the television so he didn't have to watch the tourney continue without him and his team.

Now with a piece of the net tucked in his hat, Arcidiacono, who turned 22 that night, tried to put his emotions into words.

"I didn't know what to do," he said later. "I think I ran in a complete circle. I was freaking out. It was unbelievable and something I'll always remember. It was just…it's four years of commitment to Villanova and as a program, I think it was just big-time for us."

Wright arrived at the podium an uncharacteristic mess—his hair disheveled, his shirt soaked—and he couldn't have been happier. His players had hit him with a surprise attack when he walked into the locker room, squirting him with water bottles and messing up his hair.

Though he'd insisted for years that how the Wildcats finished the season didn't matter, that he wouldn't judge his team's success on its record alone, the coach came clean about how much making the Final Four meant to him.

"Coaching is a lot like parenting," he said. "You just believe in your guys so much and you're telling them how great they can be. And you know it. You see it in them, but they're 18 to 22 years old. Sometimes they don't realize it and you get them maybe 75 percent of the way there and they leave you. You feel good for them, they got partly there, but you feel like you failed them a little bit. It's the greatest feeling in the world to see these guys get to that point where everyone else sees that they're as good as we see they can be. [In the locker room] it was a real sense of accomplishment and I think they really felt good about themselves individually. And that's the greatest thing that you can experience as a coach."

The Wildcats only had a handful of days to come down from the euphoria of making the Final Four and actually settle down to preparing for it. Villanova was scheduled to face Oklahoma, an offensive juggernaut that featured Buddy Hield, the national player of the year, in the national semifinal. On March 30, Villanova ended its final practice before heading to Houston, an even bigger crowd of fans and students surrounding the bus.

As the players headed to the showers, Ochefu called Arcidiacono back.

"We gotta kiss the V," Ochefu said.

At first Arcidiacono wasn't sure what his teammate meant. Then he realized this would be their last practice at Villanova. Kneeling side by side, the two bent down to the Davis Center practice facility court floor and kissed the huge V logo. When the picture hit social media, it immediately went viral.

Afterward, standing in the middle of a celebratory crowd, an emotional Wright talked about his seniors. Fighting back tears and his voice cracking, Wright called his senior class "incredible people."

"When those guys, when they kissed the court today, that just said it all to me," he said.

In Oklahoma and Hield, though, Villanova would face a program and a senior as revered as the Wildcats' two leaders. The ebullient Hield had owned much of the college basketball season, his megawatt smile the only thing that could match his megawatt game. Much like

Ochefu and Arcidiacono, Hield had worked himself into a great player, practicing in the gym when no one was watching, turning a onetime defensive player into the most scintillating offensive player in the country. The Bahamian averaged 25 points per game and connected on 46 percent of his three-pointers. In a regular-season triple-overtime loss to Kansas, the Jayhawks fans were so impressed by Hield, who scored 46 points, they gave their opponent a standing ovation when he left the court. The Big 12's all-time scoring leader and single-season record holder, Hield had scored 30 or more points in 10 games heading into the NCAA Tournament.

And he didn't exactly slow down in March. Through the Sooners' first four NCAA games, Hield was averaging 29.2 points per game, and was coming off an Elite Eight game where he torched Oregon for 37.

If all that weren't enough to sober Villanova, there was also this— 78–55. That was the final score when the Wildcats faced the Sooners at Pearl Harbor in December. In the humbling loss, the Wildcats' first of the season, Oklahoma connected on 14 three-pointers while Villanova shot 4-of-32. Needless to say, the loss came up in every conversation leading into the game but Wright and his players argued that the previous game actually worked in their favor. It gave them a barometer of how much work they needed to do. Both teams came into that December contest ranked in the top 10; only one stayed that way. It was cold water splashed in the Wildcats' faces, a reminder that their ranking was based more on past accomplishments than current successes.

But it also served Villanova well at the Final Four. The Wildcats knew how good Oklahoma was—as a team. As great as Hield had been all season, it was the entire Sooners team that took it to Villanova at Pearl Harbor. Five players scored in double digits against Villanova; Hield, who finished with 18, wasn't even the high scorer.

"Our guys have great respect for them," Wright said.

With two high-powered offenses going head to head and so much on the line, most everyone in college basketball anticipated a wild, high-scoring national semifinal. They were half right. There was a lot of scoring; it was just one-sided.

If there were any skeptics still questioning if Villanova belonged in the Final Four, they turned into converts on that Saturday night in Houston. What the Wildcats did to Oklahoma had quite literally never been done before. After trading bucket for bucket for the first seven minutes, Oklahoma led 17–16. That would be it for the Sooners. From that point forward, Villanova outscored Oklahoma 79–34, winning the game 95–51. The 44-point scoring gap blistered the 37-year-old record for margin of victory at a Final Four game by 10 points. The Wildcats shot 71 percent from the floor, topping another Final Four record, this one set in 1961. They scored more points in the second half (53) than Oklahoma did in the entire game.

And as near flawless as the Wildcats were offensively, they were equally good defensively. Hield finished with just nine points and ended his career on the bench, with a towel over his head.

"Got whipped in every way," is how Oklahoma coach Lon Kruger aptly described the game.

Maybe the most telling play of the game, though, came on a miss. Villanova sophomore Phil Booth drove to the hoop for a layup and was met hard at the rim but no foul was called. On the sideline, Wright lost his mind, screeching at the officials to call the foul. The Wildcats, at the time, led by 41. The coach later apologized to the official and in the press conference sheepishly admitted that, though he was worried Booth could get hurt on the play, he checked himself after looking at the score.

But the in-game reaction, really, was just a precursor of Villanova's postgame mood. Lost amid the jaw-dropping statistical mayhem of the game was the fact that the Wildcats still had one more game to play—the national championship game.

"We came here," Arcidiacono said afterward, "to win two games, not just one."

Two days later, Villanova and North Carolina faced off for the final game of the 2016 season.

Just before tipoff, Hagan gathered the Wildcats for the final time. He reminded them of a Gospel reading from John that he'd referenced frequently during the year, about the vine and branches. The message was simple—that no branch can bear fruit by itself; it must remain true to the vine. This team, he told them, had always stayed true to the vine, sacrificing individual glory for the greater good.

Just like they no longer needed clips of Rocky or the U.S. Olympic team to fire them up, Hagan explained that they no longer needed a lengthy sermon from him to remind them of why they were successful.

"Be the branches that you are, connected to the vine and taking strength, so that your life can bear fruit," he said. "Go out there and be who you are."

With 4.7 seconds left in the game, the branches spread out to their spots on the court, executing their last play together as a team.

And Jenkins let the ball fly.

Just as CBS announcer Jim Nantz shouted, "For the championship!" on the national television broadcast, setting up the would-it-or-wouldn't-it-drop drama of the final shot, Mikal Bridges made his first step up from the bench and onto the court.

The freshman decided he didn't need to wait to see if the ball would score or miss; he'd already made up his mind. Bridges boldly moved toward what he anticipated would be a buzzer-beating celebration before the ball even slipped through the net. As his teammate Jalen Brunson spread his arms wide, holding back what could be a premature court storming, Bridges threw his hands in the air and caution to the wind. He hesitated for maybe a half second after taking that first step but then immediately sprinted, the first bench player to reach Jenkins in the celebratory scrum.

"One of our coaches goes, 'That's good! That's good!'" Bridges said. "I looked and I saw it and I thought it looked good, too. I was already running on the court when it went in."

In sports, there is nothing more exciting than the dramatic finish— the walk-off home run, the Hail Mary pass, the overtime-winning goal, and, of course, the buzzer beater. Joe Montana's touchdown pass to Dwight Clark in the 1982 NFC Championship Game still lives on as "The Catch," just as Bill Mazeroski's Game 7 World Series bottom-of-the-ninth homer continues to resonate more than 50 years since he launched it.

The NCAA Tournament is built for such heroics, its win-or-go-home design injecting anxiety into every game. No surprise, then, that it's nearly cornered the market on last-second drama. From Bryce Drew's dramatic hook-and-ladder winner for Valparaiso, to Christian Laettner's turnaround jumper for Duke, to Mario Chalmers' overtime-forcing three-pointer for Kansas, to Lorenzo Charles' putback for N.C. State's stunning title win, there's a reason it's called March Madness.

The 2016 NCAA Tournament might have been the maddest of them all. Capping a turbulent season in which six different teams held the No. 1 ranking, the tourney was pure mayhem. Michigan State, one of those top-ranked teams, lost in the first round. Yale won its first tournament game in school history. Temple lost to Iowa in overtime on a putback rebound at the buzzer. Providence rallied from seven points behind to beat USC with 1.5 seconds left. In the span of mere minutes, Northern Iowa hit a halfcourt, buzzer-beating three-pointer to beat Texas in Oklahoma City, while in Spokane, Cincinnati missed on a would-be tying dunk after officials ruled it came after time expired.

Villanova's theatrical finish, then, was the absolute right end to a chaotic year.

But the tricky thing about fantastic finishes is that sometimes they mask what had been otherwise ordinary games. Exciting finishes don't always equate to well-played games. That Providence-USC game, for example, was fraught with endgame mistakes. Yet the end was so exciting the mistakes were easy to forget—and forgive.

What separated the 2016 national championship game from the pack is that from the first shot—a Joel Berry three-pointer for North Carolina—until the last, it was a taut, tension-filled drama that left fans little time to sit, let alone breathe.

"You know, there are 75 possessions in the game," North Carolina's Marcus Paige said after the loss. "They just happened to get the last one and make the shot."

It was exactly that sort of game, the sort that left people wondering what might have happened if there had been more time on the clock.

It is easy, in fact, to imagine the Tar Heels coming up with an answer because, for 40 minutes, that's what the two teams did—trade tough shot for tough shot, scoring run for scoring run.

North Carolina took its biggest lead of the game—a seven-point advantage—with 38 seconds remaining until halftime. Villanova answered in the only way it knows how—with attitude. Josh Hart chased down Justin Jackson on a would-be fast break, blocking the Tar Heel's player's shot. Ryan Arcidiacono scooped up the ball and whipped a pass to Phil Booth.

"Shoot it!" Arcidiacono yelled at Booth. The sophomore did, just before the buzzer sounded.

Without Hart's block, Villanova could have been down nine. Instead, the Wildcats trailed by just five.

Despite the furious finish to the opening 20 minutes, the Wildcats weren't happy in the locker room. They hadn't played poorly but they also didn't believe they had played as well as they could. Their defense was porous, allowing North Carolina to turn the tables on Villanova and shoot 7-of-9 from the three-point arc. Their own offense was foolish, taking more difficult shots than makeable ones, and they'd turned the ball over six times, giving the Tar Heels, a team that loved the fast break, 10 easy points.

It wasn't what they had come to Houston to do. For everyone else in the traveling party, the trip was a fun weekend, a celebratory finish to a great season. For Villanova, it was a business trip. Wright had all but sequestered his team in its hotel, avoiding as much of the hoopla as he could in and around the city. Other than practice, media obligations, and team dinners, the Wildcats essentially kept to themselves.

It was a far cry from the approach Wright had used seven years earlier, when the Wildcats played in the Final Four in Detroit. Villanova practically hosted a party every day. Patrick Chambers, now the head coach at Penn State, was an assistant on staff then. He remembered pregame meals that seemed more like banquets, with family members, friends, boosters—really anyone who wanted to come—joining the players to eat. Some people would even sit in on team meetings; during a film session, Chambers recalled Wright chatting up Vice President Joe Biden on the phone.

"It was a circus," Chambers said. "But we were so happy to be there and that was the problem. It was, 'Wow. We made the Final Four.' We didn't realize that, yeah, we made it, but we weren't done."

Remembering that experience, and even more the resulting 83–69 blowout loss to North Carolina, Chambers texted Wright before the 2016 Final Four, warning him not to make the same mistakes.

He needn't have worried. How dialed in were the Wildcats this time around? When asked after the Oklahoma game about any nerves playing in front of Vice President Biden (whose wife, Jill, received a master's degree from Villanova), Hart smiled.

"I didn't know he was here," Hart said.

Which is why the Wildcats were so frustrated at the half of the title game. They weren't playing with the focus they believed the game merited. In the locker room the coaching staff didn't even speak much; the seniors did most of the talking. Ochefu and Arcidiacono reminded their teammates of how they defined Villanova basketball and more, how they defined themselves, calling on them to meet the standards they had set for the first 39 games of the season.

Message received. As the second half began, the Wildcats got back to their roots. They connected one small act with another, stringing together the little things that collectively lead to great things, slowly chipping away at the Tar Heels' advantage.

With 16:59 to play, Brice Johnson scored on a dunk to put UNC ahead 43–38. Over the next four minutes and 15 seconds, Villanova would outscore the Heels 11–3 to retake the lead. The go-ahead exclamation point came via a Booth three-pointer, but that hero shot wasn't the game breaker. The game changed because of the stuff that doesn't show up in the box score but earns check marks in Attitude Club. North Carolina failed to score on four of its next six possessions, their shooters unable to find breathing room thanks to the Wildcats more closely contesting their shots. Their guards struggled to handle the ramped-up defense, turning the ball over twice in that span.

By the time it was all said and done, Villanova would, piece by piece, put together one of the epic runs it had become known for in this NCAA Tournament, outscoring North Carolina 27–14 to take a 10-point lead with a little more than five minutes to play.

By all rights the game should have been over at that point. North Carolina had been completely thrown off of its game. The same team that shot 53 percent in first half could connect on only 34 percent of its opportunities in the second. But like Villanova, the Tar Heels weren't disappearing without a fight.

"I was dumb enough when we were down 10, I promised 'em, if they do what I said, we'd come back and we'd have a chance to win the game at the end," North Carolina coach Roy Williams said.

That the Tar Heels believed their coach says a lot about North Carolina. That the Wildcats knew the game was far from over says even more about the quality of the game.

"When we took the 10-point lead, given how the game had gone to that point, we never expected to go up double digits," associate head coach Baker Dunleavy said. "We figured it was going to be one of those games that comes down to the wire. Even up 10, I was thinking, *This is going to be a game where we have to execute.* I was just hoping we'd be up four or five and just have to execute our press offense, not our last-second, tie-game play."

Over the next four minutes, the Tar Heels essentially did to Villanova what the Wildcats had done to them earlier. With North Carolina extending its defensive pressure, Villanova scored on just two of its next seven possessions, missing layups and jumpers and twice turning the ball over. By the time the Heels were done, they'd made it 70–69, setting up the ferocious final minute.

In most cases—in almost every case, in fact—Paige's double-pump three-pointer is the moment of the season, the highlight to be played over and over. Like Ochefu and Arcidiacono, Paige was also a senior who had endured his share of strife during his career. An academic scandal had tainted North Carolina's reputation and cast a huge shadow over the Tar Heels' entire season, the players left to answer questions about misdeeds they were not party to. The investigation pressed on for years, a slow-drip of news without a conclusion that offered little respite for Williams and his players, who were admittedly tired of dealing with it.

Paige was the bright light. A terrific student who stuck around for four years, he began his final year in the conversation for various national honors, and as the leader of a team that was favored early to win the championship. Instead he struggled all year with a shooting slump that eliminated him from award consideration and undermined the impact he could have on his own team. As North Carolina struggled to play as dominantly as people thought its talent dictated, Paige's shooting woes only amplified.

The struggles dogged him in the national championship game, too. For the first 38 minutes and 30 seconds of that game, Paige was just 4-of-12 from the floor, connecting on 2-of-5 three-point attempts. But when his team needed him most, Paige rose to the occasion. He scored eight points in the final 90 seconds, including those final three, on a shot where it appeared as if he hung in the air from a wire.

"I've coached a lot of guys, but I've never coached anybody any tougher than that kid," Williams said of Paige. "I've never coached anybody that tried to will things to happen even when he wasn't playing as well as he could play."

By all rights, then, Paige should have been the star of the show. Instead he is a footnote to history, the would-be hero forgotten and swept up with the detritus of Villanova's celebration.

As Jenkins' shot went in, Paige, along with senior teammate Brice Johnson, were the closest guys to the basket. The ball literally and cruelly fell through the net and bounced between the two of them. Paige immediately threw his palms upward as if to say, "What can you do?" before making his way off the court with his stunned teammates.

"When you're a kid growing up you don't dream of missing the last-second shot or you don't dream of a team beating you at the buzzer," Paige said afterward. "You dream of having that moment, that confetti, seeing your family over there crying tears of joy, hugging the guys you gave blood, sweat, and tears with for four years. That's what you dream of. And we were this close to that dream."

For so many others, though, Jenkins' shot was the dream come true.

For Villanova fans, for people even tangentially connected to the program, the second Jenkins' shot went in became a where-were-you moment. In corner bars and at office cubicles, on talk radio and in school classrooms, people felt compelled to share their own story of that final shot.

Weeks and even months later, they continued to stop Jenkins—fellow students and grandparents, wealthy businessmen and little kids—to tell him what they remembered from the moment he secured Villanova's national championship.

"I understand we won the national championship," Jenkins said. "But honestly, I don't think I'll understand the magnitude of that shot until I'm done playing basketball."

From NRG Stadium to the East Coast, and all the way to France, what people remember, how they reacted, and what they felt after sums up maybe better than anything what this Villanova championship meant to so many. For some programs, programs that expect to be in this position with regularity, winning a title is almost a relief. It is to be savored, certainly, but more a catharsis for having delivered what had been demanded.

For teams such as Villanova, national programs that expect to succeed but exist outside the rarefied air of constant scrutiny, it's different. It's not that the Wildcats and their fans don't believe they can and should win national championships. They just have an appreciation for how hard it is to do, and how rare the opportunity is.

Villanova last won a national title in 1985. The reactions to Jenkins' shot, then, were 31 years in the making.

From France

It was 5:00 in the morning in Le Mans, France, and Mouphtaou Yarou didn't care if he was waking the neighbors. As he watched Jenkins take the last shot, he started screaming. As a former Villanova basketball player, Yarou knew exactly what the Wildcats were going to do. He learned the play, Nova, when he was on the roster and knew how it was designed to work.

Yarou also recognized immediately that North Carolina had made a fatal mistake.

"I saw two guys follow Arch and they left Kris open," Yarou said. "I knew it was going in. He's a great shooter."

Yarou enjoyed a one-man celebration in his apartment, then sent a quick text to Wright and to Ochefu, who he had mentored years earlier. Finally, he FaceTimed Frank Kelly. The former Maryland senator and Villanova graduate (Class of 1961) has been a father figure since Yarou emigrated to the United States from Benin in 2007. Kelly was in NRG Stadium.

"I was jumping around and screaming," Yarou said. "I almost got in trouble."

From Oklahoma City, Oklahoma

Billy Donovan is no stranger to either college basketball pressure or drama. He led the University of Florida to back-to-back national championships. The first time, in 2006, no one saw Florida coming. Like Villanova, the Gators had been dogged by early losses in the NCAA Tournament. Since an appearance in the 2000 title game, they'd lost five consecutive times in the first weekend. His 2006 team was young and though a No. 3 seed, not necessarily a hot pick to win it all. Instead, outside of a four-point win against Georgetown in the Sweet 16, Florida dismantled everyone in its path—including Villanova in the Elite Eight—to win the national title.

A year later, with the bulk of its roster returning, everything was different. The carefree team from the year before nearly caved to the pressure of expectations. In some ways that championship was sweeter. No one had won back-to-back titles since Duke in 1992. But it was also less enjoyable, feeling more like work than playing a game.

So Donovan knew how each coach was feeling in the title game. Villanova, the underdog, was his team in 2006. North Carolina, the blueblood without a title since 2009, was his 2007 squad.

But the coach had left college basketball that season and was deep into a new challenge of his own. In April 2015 he'd stunned the college community by taking the head coaching job with the NBA's Oklahoma City Thunder. He was between road games on national championship Monday, so engrossed in studying film before the Thunder's game against the Denver Nuggets that he was only half paying attention.

"I watched the first half," Donovan said. "But Villanova went up 10 and I turned it off."

A few minutes later his phone blipped with an alert, telling him about Paige's tying three.

"I flipped on the TV and saw the last play," Donovan said.

Later, everyone would remark in wonder at Arcidiacono's selflessness, how the four-year captain and the guy most everyone in the building thought would take the shot, instead dished the pass to Jenkins. Donovan wasn't the least bit surprised. He'd recruited Arcidiacono heavily, recognizing in the point guard the intangibles that make more than a good player; the ones, instead, that make a winner.

"Winning for Ryan has always been first and foremost," Donovan said. "He understood to achieve what he wants to achieve as a player, he had to win at a high level. It's so easy for a coach to say to a kid he's not athletic enough or big enough but with someone like Ryan, you can't take him off the floor because your chance of winning is impacted. He's going to make the winning play and in that situation, he made the winning play. Regardless of whether the shot went in, Ryan understood what he had to do to give his team a chance to win. I was so very, very happy for him."

From Newport, Rhode Island

Mike Tranghese has been watching basketball games in an official capacity for the better part of 40 years. He stood alongside the legendary Dave Gavitt when the Big East Conference was formed and later took over the reins of the conference himself. He knows the game, knows its nuances and tics. He also knows Villanova. He was in charge of the Big East back when the Wildcats won the national championship in 1985.

And he knows, above all else, how coaches think.

"They all say the same thing—spread the floor and get the ball in the hands of the best player," Tranghese said.

He thought back to the early 1970s, back when Gavitt was the head coach at Providence College and the Big East not even an idea in his head. In 1973 the Friars rode the coattails of Ernie DiGregorio all the way to the Final Four. DiGregorio—Ernie D to his fans—was a dynamic player and a showman whose deft passes left fans in awe of his skills.

"Dave would say, 'Don't call a timeout,'" Tranghese remembered. "He'd yell, 'Get the ball in Ernie D's hands and get out of the way.'"

Tranghese wasn't at the championship game. He was home in Newport, recovering from appendicitis, but even from that far away, he knew that Wright would do exactly what Gavitt did all those years ago—get the ball in the hands of his best player and get out of the way.

"Ryan was there for four years. He was trained for that moment," Tranghese said. "As soon as I saw it, I knew it had a chance. I knew Kris had that kind of range."

From Old Westbury, New York

Overtime—the game was headed to overtime. Speedy Claxton wasn't one to track in pessimism, but as a former basketball player and now a coach, he was a realist. And when a kid hits a crazy shot like Paige just did, the basketball gods don't allow for a trump card.

"And I thought if it went to overtime, North Carolina was going to win," said Claxton, who played for Wright at Hofstra. "I was sitting in my house, shaking my head, saying, 'This is going to be tough.'"

But once he saw how the Tar Heels intended to defend Villanova's last shot, Claxton changed his mind. He realized they weren't guarding the inbounder—Jenkins—and he also knew how good a shooter Jenkins was. When he saw how wide open Jenkins was on the play, the pessimistic realist turned into an immediate optimist.

"I started standing up as soon as he let it fly," Claxton said. "I knew it looked good once it left his hand."

From Hatboro, Pennsylvania

Mike Mikulski didn't think he was nervous. Sitting at home watching the game, he knew he was excited in the final minutes but nervous? No. He was fine.

And then he looked at his wrist.

"We all wear these FitBits now," he said. "I realized I was sitting on my sofa and my pulse was up like around 100. My resting heart rate is supposed to be in the mid-50s."

An athlete himself and once a Division III coach for 13 years, Mikluski was smart enough not to relax when Villanova pushed its lead to 10 points. Five minutes in college basketball, he knew, was an eternity. And as North Carolina made one impossible shot after another, he admitted he started to wonder. The Wildcats were playing good defense in his estimation but it was like the pendulum was purposefully swinging away from Villanova, almost guiding the Tar Heels' shots into the basket.

But he also trusted Wright, his childhood buddy who even as a kid never seemed unnerved. He believed that Villanova would at least get a chance to win the game. In his wildest dreams, though, he couldn't have conjured that finish.

"I just couldn't believe it," he said. "I was almost relieved."

So relieved and overwhelmed, in fact, Mikulski broke his own cardinal rule. He purposefully tries to avoid texting or calling Wright unless absolutely necessary, knowing how busy the coach is, and also knowing that no matter how much time goes by, the two will pick up their lifelong friendship when they reconnect.

But he couldn't help himself. Amid the chaos and the excitement, he instinctively reached for his phone.

"I texted him right away," Mikulski said. "He got back to me eventually, but it took a couple of days."

From Newtown, Pennsylvania

With four kids ranging in age from one to 11, Derek Wright figured his own crowd would be every bit as entertaining as the one assembled at NRG Stadium. So when his brother called to offer him a lift via a private plane to watch the championship game, Derek declined, settling in with his wife and kids instead for a viewing party.

The family was having a grand time, the kids romping around and cheering as Villanova extended its lead to 10 points. As a basketball coach himself, Derek knew that the lead was fool's gold. He fully expected North Carolina to make a run and when the Tar Heels mounted their comeback, he saw it as most coaches would—as the typical ebb and flow of a game.

His kids didn't quite see it the same way.

"They were literally crying," Derek said. "I'm like, 'I'm telling you, we're gonna win this game.' They didn't buy it."

The kids especially doubted their dad's faith after Paige hit the tying shot. Whether it was a premonition or coaching instinct, Derek still believed the Wildcats would win. When the NCAA Tournament bracket was revealed, he thought the regional final against Kansas would be their most arduous task. Once Villanova passed that test, he felt in his gut his brother's team would win it all.

As the Wildcats huddled during the timeout and his kids wailed, Derek also realized that 4.7 seconds was more than enough time to get off a good shot. Derek also knew exactly what play his brother would call. As the head coach at Council Rock South High School, Derek runs a derivative of Nova, too. It's easier, he joked, to be successful when you have Division I athletes and not high school kids. Still, he knows that the way the play is designed, with so many options, is a terrific last-second setup.

And since he'd known Arcidiacono all the way back to middle school, he knew Villanova had the perfect quarterback to execute the play.

Typically Derek is like a lot of coaches, so caught up in the moment of a game he doesn't allow himself time to celebrate it. But this time he wasn't a coach and he wasn't on the sideline. He was a brother, sitting in his living room with his kids and his wife.

When Jenkins' shot went in, he celebrated as loudly as they did.

"It was crazy," he said, shaking his head. "Just crazy."

From Newtown Square, Pennsylvania

Billy Lange's house sounded a lot like Derek Wright's—four crying kids distraught that their Wildcats were losing.

"'Oh, they're gonna lose, they're gonna lose,' that's what they were all saying," said Lange, Wright's former assistant who is now on staff with the 76ers. "I kept telling them, 'It's all right.'"

Even after Paige hit the tying shot, Lange merely shrugged his shoulders.

"Oh, I figured that was going to happen," he said. "That's part of the drama."

By the time Villanova broke the huddle, though, Lange was getting anxious himself. He was behind his sofa, pacing back and forth. A good friend of Wright's, he'd also been on the staff when the coach recruited a number of players on the current roster. He felt like he was watching his own kids play.

But he also knew those kids pretty well, especially Jenkins. He made more than a few trips to Maryland to woo Jenkins to Villanova. Lange had watched him play high school games and summer-league games, saw him not just make big shots but fearlessly continue to take them.

When he saw that it was Jenkins taking the last shot he started walking from behind his couch toward his wife, Alicia.

"I knew," he said, "it was going in."

174

From NRG Stadium, Houston, Texas
Val Ackerman

She was there when the Dream Team won the gold medal in Barcelona in 1992 and when the United States women captured gold in Atlanta in 1996. In London in 2012, she attended no less than 27 Olympic basketball games.

And yet when Val Ackerman ranks the top basketball games she's seen in her career, she puts Villanova's 2016 national championship triumph right near the top. It may sound self-serving. Ackerman is, after all, the commissioner of the Big East Conference and the Wildcats' title legitimized her league. But Ackerman is also a basketball connoisseur. Among the first female athletes to earn a scholarship to the University of Virginia and the school's first 1,000-point scorer, she knows good hoops when she sees it.

She also knows drama.

"That was one of the most riveting games I've ever sat through," Ackerman said.

It was also, she admits, one of the most exhausting. At one point, Ackerman was caught in a picture with her head down on the press table in front of her, clearly agonized by the back and forth of the game. When it was over Ackerman said she felt "emotionally drained," and as she looked around, thought everyone looked the same.

"There was a moment of—the immediate reaction was just being stunned," Ackerman said. "Stunned that it happened, stunned how it happened. People were just soaking in the moment."

Ackerman stayed in the arena until well past midnight. She attended the postgame press conferences and visited with Wright briefly. She had attended five of the Wildcats' six NCAA games and knew how much the win meant to Wright, to the program, and to her conference.

"It was an amazing run," she said. "Just exhilarating."

Joe Arcidiacono

Sitting in the Villanova section diagonally across from the Wildcats bench, Joe Arcidiacono got swept up in the moment. In a building louder and more rambunctious than he can remember being in, surrounded by his wife and kids, a guy who played sports his entire life and was a regular either coaching or watching his children compete made the biggest rookie mistake of his life.

"We took that 10-point lead and I let my guard down," Joe said. "I was like, 'Holy crap, we're going to win this thing!'"

And then as Carolina stormed back, bit by bit, Joe cursed himself. By the time Paige knotted the score, he figured he'd jinxed his son, Ryan, so badly he'd all but cost the Wildcats the game.

"I'm like, 'He tied the freaking game on that shot?'" Joe said. "The legs all over the place? It was crazy."

Steeling himself for the heartbreaking finish, trying to imagine what words he could possibly offer to console his son, Joe broke yet another rule. He forgot the old Yogi Berra adage—it ain't over til it's over.

Still stunned by Paige's make he nearly fell over when Jenkins' shot slipped through the net. He can't remember quite what he did—kissed his wife and hugged his other kids, for sure—but he remembers what he yelled over and over again.

"Did we just win it? Did we just win it?" Joe said. "There's no way. There's no way we just did this."

Seth Berger

When Seth Berger found his seat at the KFC Yum! Center in Louisville a week earlier, he immediately befriended the group of guys sitting in the row in front of him. They were all buddies of George Halcovage, Wright's director of basketball operations. So when Berger and his two boys got to their seats in Houston, he was excited to see the same group of guys sitting nearby.

"Only they were sitting behind me this time," said Berger, Ochefu's high school coach. "I said, "Should we switch? I don't want to jinx things.""

They rolled the dice, figuring their seat locations probably wouldn't directly impact the game's outcome. As North Carolina shredded Villanova's 10-point lead, there might have been a little second guessing of that decision.

But Berger had no such doubts as he watched Jenkins go up to shoot. He had a terrific angle, sitting directly across from the North Carolina bench and right in line with the Villanova basket.

"I've watched enough games and I had the right angle," Berger said. "I knew it was good. One hundred percent knew it."

Nate Britt Sr.

How did Nate Britt Sr. react to Jenkins' shot? Alas, there's photographic evidence.

The entire Britt family spent the championship game splitting their allegiances between North Carolina, where their biological son, Nate, played, and Villanova, where Jenkins, the boy they'd come to raise as their own, played.

Britt Sr. went so far as to change his T-shirt and his seat assignment in the second half, swapping out his Villanova dark blue for Carolina blue. He was meant, of course, to be cheering for the Tar Heels in those final seconds. It was their turn.

But the game was too epic and the finish too unbelievable to hold true to any scripted behavior. As Jenkins rose for the shot, Britt knew him well enough to know where the ball was going and he immediately stood to his feet and thrust his hands overhead.

"Both hands went up," he said. "And there's a picture of it, of me in my Carolina shirt celebrating with all of these upset Carolina fans around me. I was a little embarrassed. My brother said, 'Dang, you're on the Carolina side doing that?' But what could I do?"

Father Rob Hagan

He should have had one of the best seats in the house. He was on the team bench, after all. But thanks to the elevated courts at the Final Four, the bench actually sits below floor level, so anyone sitting there must constantly look up to see the action. Plus, the Wildcats bench was at the opposite end—a full 94 feet away—from their basket and Father Rob Hagan was at the very end of that bench.

So he couldn't quite see where Jenkins' shot was headed but he had faith it would go in. And not just because he's a man of the cloth. Hagan had sat in on countless Villanova practices in the last three seasons, watched them run their final play, and more important, had watched Jenkins shoot.

"From my angle I couldn't see, but I knew he was money ball," Hagan said. "Since the day he set foot on campus, Kris has been the best shooter on our team."

The enormity of what happened didn't really connect with Hagan immediately. The confetti falling from the arena ceiling, the players dogpiling at midcourt, made some impact but it wasn't until a long time later, when Hagan went in the locker room, that he really appreciated it.

The players were seated at their lockers, most of them on their phones, many checking out the various YouTube videos of fans reacting to the shot. The Wildcats had been so focused on their one-game, next-game mentality that Hagan got swept up in it, too.

"When it was finally over, that's when it hit me," Hagan said. "Wow! This is really a big deal."

Felicia Jenkins

It was silent, or at least it seemed that way. As her son rose to decide the outcome of the 2016 national championship game, Felicia Jenkins heard absolutely nothing. Certainly people had to be making noise—cheering or screaming or something. But as Jenkins, a former basketball player herself and now a high school coach, stood in a defensive crouch, she couldn't hear it.

"I could hear people breathe in, almost as if they were all inhaling, and waiting to exhale," she said. "I knew there would be cheering if he missed or if he made it. Either way the place was going to erupt but I couldn't hear anything."

When the shot went in, when her son cemented himself as a March hero, Jenkins leapt into the arms of Robin Booth, whose son, Phil, scored 20 points in the title game. Neither woman could hold the other up and they wound up falling in a mosh pit of glee. The tears quickly followed and then Felicia started moving. She bounded down the steps to the court, desperate to get to her son. A security guard foolishly tried to stop her.

"No, no, no," Felicia said. "I'm going across. Get out of the way."

As she tried to get past the yellow-jacketed guard, Felicia's son caught her eye. He made his way over to his mother and the security guard quickly disappeared. When Jenkins was close enough, Felicia made another leap. This time her son caught her and held on.

"Outside of him being born, that was the most amazing feeling I've ever had," Felicia said. "To share that with your son, to know all the work he's put in has paid off, I can't even describe it."

Joe Jones

From his seat in the middle of the stadium, just to the left of the basket where Villanova would take its last shot, Joe Jones, Wright's former assistant and now the head coach at Boston University, was thinking one thing.

What is that dude doing?

To that point nothing had surprised Jones. Not that the Wildcats were in the national championship game. Not that North Carolina had fought back from a 10-point hole late in the game. Not even Paige's crazy last shot.

"As a coach, you're used to crazy things happening," he said. "I'm numb to that."

But a starting player grabbing a mop just before the last play of the national title game? *That* Jones had never seen. Once he got past the confusion and really looked at Ochefu, he was even more stunned.

"He looked so relaxed," Jones said.

He took that as a sign that the Wildcats weren't overwhelmed by the moment, and they'd be able to execute something down the stretch. Jones might have been the only person in the building who didn't expect Arcidiacono to take the final shot. As an ex-assistant under Wright, he sort of recognized the play. They'd always run something similar, even back in their days at Hofstra, and so he understood that a hard drive to the basket was an option.

But he didn't see Arcidiacono making that play.

Then again, he didn't see him passing to Jenkins, either.

"From watching him play for so long, I felt like he'd bring the ball up, draw someone in, and then kick it," Jones said. "But I thought he'd give it to Booth because he'd scored so much in the game."

Which is how Jones, a coach by trade and a longtime part of the Villanova family, came to be as stunned as so many others in the building when Jenkins took and made the shot. A friend sitting next to him snapped a picture of a joyful Jones, his arms up above his head, with a look of pure wonder on his face. He still has the picture and has no intention of getting rid of it.

"It's this unbelievable, surreal feeling that I still can't describe," Jones said a good four months after the championship game. "Jay is family. Villanova is family. I didn't know those kids but I felt the connection to the program and it was just, I don't know, this feeling I can't even describe that you only get to experience so many times in your life."

Kyle Lowry

The Toronto Raptors were playing the next day, at home against Charlotte, and the Houston-to-Toronto commute isn't exactly a short one. Kyle Lowry didn't care. Fresh off of his first All-Star appearance, the former Villanova guard wasn't about to miss his Wildcats play for a national championship.

So less than 24 hours before his own game, Lowry took his seat directly behind Wright's wife, Patty, just behind the Villanova bench.

He knew the play the Wildcats would run and when he saw Jenkins get the ball, he also knew he'd make it. Lowry spends his off-season back home in Philadelphia and uses the Villanova practice facility for training. He frequently works out with the returning Wildcats and spent more than a few days with Jenkins in the summer before the season started.

"Do you know how many times I've seen that kid take that shot in the summer? At least 1,000," Lowry said after the game. "I knew it was going in."

Vince Nicastro

As Villanova's athletic director, Vince Nicastro had a floor pass tucked in his pocket for the championship game. With a few minutes left, he made his way from his seat 20 rows up in the Villanova fan section to a media table in the end zone opposite the Wildcats' basket.

It wasn't exactly the greatest view.

"You're so far away, so it's like, 'Did that just happen?'" said Nicastro, who is now the associate commissioner at the Big East Conference.

The euphoria on the court afterward drove it home. His wife, Liz, was bawling and hugging everyone she could find. Lost in the midst of the on-court crowd Nicastro found Brian Murray. A Villanova associate athletic director and a graduate of the school, Jim attended the 1985 game as a kid with his father. Jim Murray, once the Philadelphia Eagles general manager and the founder of the Ronald McDonald House, is also a Villanova grad. He memorably drove more than an hour from Lexington, Kentucky, site of the 1985 Final Four, to the Gethsemani Abbey, a Trappist monastery, to say a few prayers before the Wildcats played Georgetown. Jim's prayers were answered that day.

Brian enjoyed a second chance to rejoice in 2016.

"He and his dad had been Villanova fans forever," Nicastro said. "And Brian was just running around crying like a baby."

Elizabeth Ochefu

It wasn't merely that Elizabeth Ochefu couldn't watch the final play of the game. She couldn't stand. She didn't trust her legs, certain she'd crumble from her nerves. And so while everyone in the building got to their feet, Elizabeth stayed rooted to her seat.

Her eyes cast down at her own feet, she closed her eyes and prayed. Except she didn't ask for a win, not in so many words.

"I was just hoping for the best," she said. "What I thought at that last moment, I thought that I think they've learned how to handle a loss. I know they're hungry and humble and I just hope they can draw on their experiences from the last four years no matter what happens."

Elizabeth never saw her son, Daniel, mop the floor, never saw Arcidiacono dribble up the court, and never saw Jenkins shoot it. She only knew the game had ended because she could feel the stadium trembling under her feet.

When she finally found the courage to look up, the fans surrounding her blocked her view. She couldn't even see the big screen. Finally she looked next to her, to her husband, Hassan.

"He was jumping up and down and smiling," Elizabeth said. "That's when I knew. I will never forget that."

John Shackleton

Like Hagan, John Shackleton was tucked at the end of the bench, struggling to see the last shot.

Rather than try to imagine what was going on, the team's strength and conditioning coach opted to look up, watching the live event playing out in front of him on the big screen. No one knew better than Shackleton the amount of work that Jenkins had put in. The two had worked on aerobic training and diet, remaking Jenkins' entire body to improve his play.

Shackleton was thrilled that Jenkins was the kid who got the last shot, that the sacrifices the player had made would receive the ultimate payoff.

But as the shot went in and everyone went crazy, Shackleton doesn't exactly know what he felt.

"I don't really think I can explain it," he said. "It was just—I don't know. It was just unreal. I know one thing. I wasn't as relaxed as Coach Wright."

Indeed, of all the crazy celebrations and giddy joy that sprung to life from literally across the globe, the ultimate reaction was best summed up in one syllable.

"Bang."

When Marquette won the national championship in 1977, head coach Al McGuire sat on the bench and wept.

After Lorenzo Charles stunned the world with an airball-catch-and-release winner over Houston in 1983, Jim Valvano frantically ran around the court, searching for someone—anyone—to hug.

In the 2016 title game, maybe the only thing more stunning than Kris Jenkins' buzzer beater was the reaction of the winning head coach.

As Jenkins' shot dropped through the net, cameras caught Jay Wright, his eyes following the track of the ball, mouth one word:

"Bang."

"Who is cooler than that?" his former Hofstra star Speedy Claxton asked.

In bars across Philadelphia and at Villanova's on-campus watch party, people erupted with joy. Around the country, people with no rooting interest whatsoever in the game still reacted to the improbability of the finish. One YouTube video showed a man in a Duke jersey, perhaps hoping only that the Tar Heels not win, scream as if the Blue Devils were the new champions. An NRG Stadium security guard, a guy paid to keep his cool, was caught on camera mouthing, "Oh my God," his eyes growing wide like saucers. On the CBS postgame stage, analyst Charles Barkley, who had no dog in the fight, jumped up and down in giddy joy, and in the stands, even Carolina grad Michael Jordan smiled and nodded his head in deference to the unbelievable finish.

It was the sort of epic end that challenged even impartial journalists to keep their cool. CBS sideline reporter Tracy Wolfson posted an image of herself to Instagram, standing at her press table seat, mouth agape.

Meantime, Wright sauntered by in front of her, barely raising an eyebrow, and calling the shot with a confidence that rivaled Babe Ruth signaling his center-field home run in Game 3 of the 1932 World Series.

"Bang."

"How do you respond like that? What's wrong with him?" an astounded Carissa Wright shouted in her living room to her husband, Derek, about his big brother.

Sitting in the stands, Joe Jones knew the answer. Wright's former assistant watched the coach's reaction and immediately started laughing. Some 20 years earlier, Hofstra point guard Darius Burton scored on a running layup at the buzzer. Jones can't remember who the opponent was—he thinks it might have been Northeastern—but he vividly remembers everyone's reaction.

"Bedlam," he said.

The players rushed the court and the assistant coaches practically tackled one another in euphoria. When they finally separated and started to adjust their crooked ties and disheveled sports jackets, they saw Wright, the head coach, standing at the foul line looking back at his staff.

"We come out of the scrum and he's laughing at us," Jones said. "It was just a regular-season game, but we were all so young and we're going crazy, and he's just standing there laughing. Absolutely laughing at us, like, 'What is wrong with you guys?' The man has ice water in his veins."

The Internet apparently thought the same of Wright. Radio personality Chris Vernon tweeted, "OK, Jay Wright really is a gangster."

"There's cool and then there's Jay Wright," opened a blog from the *Washington Post*.

"Jay Wright is the coolest guy on the planet right now," penned a *Los Angeles Times* reporter.

It should be noted that the ice water did eventually thaw. Minutes after the game ended, as he embraced his wife and three kids, Wright allowed himself a smile, a grin that didn't leave his face for the entirety of the postgame celebration. He returned the bear hug from Father Peter Donohue, the Villanova president, with equal amounts of force, and later, wrapped Ryan Arcidiacono in a long, emotional embrace. Finally, he slung his arm around his mentor, Rollie Massimino, as he escorted the only other coach to win a national championship at Villanova onto the court.

The whole time, though, Wright kept shaking his head.

"Can you believe this?" he said as he cut across the court.

Sitting in his on-campus office days after the championship game, Wright still hadn't come to grips with it all. For days he woke up with the same panicky feeling, worried he hadn't prepared well enough to beat North Carolina. "You know when you have a bad dream and you wake up and you think, *Thank God that didn't actually happen*, and you get a sigh of relief?" Wright said. "This is, *Wow. We actually did beat them. It's over.*"

He knew the dream had come true. He was thrilled but he couldn't grasp the enormity of the all. It felt, he said, like he'd just won a big game, not the *biggest* game.

He also knew his reaction, or lack thereof, had caused quite a stir. Wright explained that whenever there's an attempt at a game-winning shot, he always says, "Bang," if it's his team trying to win it and "No way," if it's the opponent.

"I thought I said it in my head," he said. "I didn't realize I moved my lips."

He also said he was worried that, despite the confetti pouring down from above, either the shot came too late or the officials might add a few tenths of a second and give Carolina one last chance to tie the game.

"When you're a coach, you're always thinking about the next play," Wright said in the postgame news conference. "I was really thinking, *Is there going to be more time on the clock?* I'm the adult. I got all these 18- and 22-year-olds around me. They're going to go crazy, and I'm going to have to get them gathered up here and we're going to have to defend a play with .7 seconds. That's what I was thinking."

His friends and relatives knew, too, that Wright would never want to seem like a classless winner. Even in the midst of his own excitement he would be aware of the parallel amounts of misery Roy Williams was feeling. In fact after he said "Bang," Wright merely turned around and headed down the sideline to shake Williams' hand. Only a bum rush from his staff slowed him down.

"He's been that way for 54 years, so I'm not at all surprised," former assistant Billy Lange said. "I was only wondering if someone would be able to mess up his hair."

For the record, no one did.

In the afterglow of glory, what no one fully understood was the enormity of that shot and the ripple effects Villanova's victory would have on the entire sport of college basketball.

Villanova has been part of two of the more incredible title games. In so many ways, the two teams, as well as the two championship runs, are so utterly different that the constant questions to the 2016 Wildcats about the 1985 Wildcats seemed contrived, if not downright silly. The 1985 team was a No. 8 seed; the 2016 squad a No. 2 seed.

One lost 10 regular-season games; the other just five. One was never ranked; one held the top spot for three weeks in February. One was coached by a man who would best be described as eternally rumpled; the other led by a man who is never mussed.

Dig beneath the statistics, though, and the similarities are there—who the players were, how the two teams played, and the impact their championships created.

"That connection would be the moral," said Fox Sports analyst Bill Raftery. "Rollie was all huggy, lovey, family, and I think these [2016] kids had the same thing. The more I was around them, the more I got the feeling that they really cared for one another. Nobody cared who scored. Individually I think their team exceeded what people thought but collectively, it was extraordinary. That's what the '85 team did."

It's no surprise, really, that the two are cut of the same cloth. Wright grew up idolizing Villanova and Massimino. They were "his team" when he was a kid, and even as he grew into the head coach, that championship crew retained its mystique for him.

"That team, that 1985 team, they're almost like a fairy tale," Wright said.

Cinderella, to be exact. From unknowns to the belles of the ball, that 1985 team became instant legends as it not only won an unexpected title, but ousted Georgetown in the process. Theirs is one of the instant classics that has stood the test of time, as unbelievable now as it was then.

But that game created an aura for more than just that particular team. It forged an identity for the entire Villanova program. The Wildcats were the little engine that could, the scrappy underdogs.

No matter what the Wildcats did over the ensuing years, they could never shake it entirely. It rankled some people, fans and alumni who believed Villanova, as it asserted itself into the national landscape, should be mentioned among the basketball bluebloods. And it was a tricky fit for Steve Lappas, the coach who succeeded Massimino. As good as his teams were, as much as he raised the program's profile with players such as Tim Thomas and Kerry Kittles, he could never match his old coach's singular success.

It was different for Wright. Unlike Lappas, he was not the coach who succeeded The Coach. He was afforded the gift of time and space, and inherited a fan base more concerned with resuscitating the program rather than trying to match past glory. When he arrived on campus, in fact, the relationship between past and present had all but fractured. Where once the program couldn't escape that 1985 shadow, then it could barely celebrate it.

Villanova had been cast as the villain in the demise of the Big 5, the Philadelphia city series of round-robin games. Concerned with an NCAA mandate that was cutting the schedule back to 27 games, Massimino insisted his team simply did not have enough dates to play all of the city games. That turned the coach into persona non grata. The rift between city and coach grew so deep that Massimino eventually hightailed it out of town, taking a job at UNLV and later, another one at Cleveland State. When Lappas, one of his assistants, was named his successor, rather than view it as a continuation of his legacy, the old coach considered it a betrayal from one of his own. For years he avoided Villanova, refusing to show up whenever the 1985 team was honored.

But Wright considers Massimino not just a mentor but also a father figure. He feels indebted to the man for giving him a job at Villanova, and later recommending him for the Hofstra gig. When he succeeded Lappas—with his old coach's blessing—Wright worked to heal old wounds and bridge the chasm of animosity.

By 2005, when Villanova hung a banner to commemorate the 20th anniversary of the championship, Massimino was there for its unveiling, the first time he'd been back in an official capacity. Since then he's been a regular, his past intrinsically tied to Villanova's present. At the 2016 Final Four, nine of the 1985 Wildcats, including most outstanding player Ed Pinckney, sat in Section 109 of NRG Stadium. Massimino sat with Wright's family, directly behind the team bench.

This was about more than just Massimino. Wright recognized the importance of his program's history, that when done properly, marrying past success to the present day creates a perception of sustained excellence. And so, though his players weren't even a twitch of a twinkle in their parents' eyes in 1985, he's ensured that they've been well educated on who came before them. The old guard are regulars at games, the short-short-wearing players of the past familiar faces to the baggy-shorted generation.

And while it may not have been his goal at the time, by examining Villanova's past, Wright found his own team's future. When the coach decided he needed to retreat from the path he was headed down after the 2009 Final Four, he followed a route paved first by Massimino.

"How they want players to play, how they expect them to behave, who they want them to be, there are a lot of similarities between the two," said Pinckney.

Massimino did not build his team on superstars, nor did he sell post-college pro dreams. He sold family, telling stories about his own childhood as the youngest son of an Italian immigrant, promising players they'd have pasta dinners together just as he did growing up. Parents loved it, turning their kids over to the rumpled-looking man with ease.

Rumpled and Wright will never coexist in a sentence but the younger coach's message and methods were no different. Pinckney said Massimino loved nothing more than to show up in his dorm room unannounced, not because he was spying but because he genuinely wanted to know what his players were up to. When Pinckney later worked for Wright as an assistant, the head coach constantly peppered his assistants with questions about his players' lives—schoolwork, significant others, all of it—and, sure enough, just like Massimino, he loved to drop by the dorms.

Massimino, like Wright, targeted blue-collar kids, kids from backgrounds like his own. At the big Five Star camp in the Poconos one year, while other coaches were rightly salivating over Ewing, Chris Mullins, Karl Malone, and Charles Barkley, Massimino gravitated toward Gary McLain, Dwayne McClain, and Pinckney, all talented but slightly further down the recruiting ladder. Each, though, had an attribute that Massimino—and later Wright—loved.

"I didn't realize how tough these guys were until I started to watch them play more," said Pinckney, who was an assistant to Wright from 2003 to 2007. "Tough—that's a word Coach Mass always used with us. They both want tough kids."

Where the two teams diverged, though, was on the court.

The 1985 Wildcats were a true Cinderella, cast there by the makeup of their team.

The 2016 Wildcats were long shots, their circumstances created by the new reality and evolution of their sport.

"This Villanova team," said longtime *Philadelphia Daily News* reporter Dick Jerardi, "was a complete outlier."

The Wildcats were in 1985, too, but in an entirely different way.

By 1985, Cinderella had long enjoyed a starring role in college basketball. In 1950, the same year that the Disney movie about the charwoman turned princess debuted, City College of New York, a team made up of scrappy New York playground stars, upset the power teams of the day to win both the NIT and NCAA titles. The team's victory, coinciding with the popular movie, made for an easy comparison.

The perpetual search for the glass slipper was on, with various teams finding a good fit over the years. Just two years before Villanova claimed the crown, Jim Valvano and N.C. State collaborated for a title that has retained its place in the "One Shining Moment" highlight reel.

Circumstances and opportunity collided almost poetically for the Wildcats in 1985. That year the NCAA expanded its tournament field to 64 teams, the latest in a series of small incremental increases that signified the burgeoning interest in the college game. Only six years earlier, just 40 teams were invited to the Big Dance. The tournament was ripe for a great story and Villanova would provide it.

That year, too, the Big East announced itself as a basketball power. Still in its infancy, the conference earned six bids (out of nine teams) and two were awarded with a top seed—St. John's and defending national champion Georgetown. Three would make it to the Final Four in a show of dominance that remains unmatched.

Georgetown, though, was the real story. A year after winning the title and rolling to a 34–3 record, the Hoyas were 30–2 and, with Patrick Ewing, the most dominant player in the nation in his senior season, the prohibitive favorite to win the crown. Led by John Thompson, their outspoken and bombastic coach, Georgetown had an almost villainous appeal, a tough team that cared little what people thought of it. Years earlier a *Washington Post* reporter coined the phrase "Hoya Paranoia," a tweak at Georgetown fans who were convinced their school never got the respect it deserved. With Thompson in charge, the phrase took on new meaning. The team was aggressive and the coach prickly and neither apologized for their behavior.

In truth some of it was an act. If people expected Georgetown to behave a certain way, then Thompson figured, why fight it? Instead he used it to his advantage, letting people create mystery around his program where none existed. At the 1984 Final Four in Seattle, media members were convinced that the less-than-media-friendly Thompson had secreted his team off to an undisclosed far-off hotel, perhaps even in Canada. In truth the Hoyas walked off the bus and crossed the street, checking in to a downtown hotel.

"I didn't like being the evil empire, but I marketed it," Thompson said in 2013. "If you had an empty room and you told everybody don't go in it, it immediately gives that room value. So when we started to say we're not going to do this or do that—hell, nobody was writing about us before that."

Villanova was everything Georgetown wasn't. Seeded eighth, the Wildcats were a nice team made up of decent players but no obvious superstars. Massimino was no less a personality than Thompson, but the disheveled Italian came off as more a harmless, happy clown than the menacing man with the towel slung over his shoulder.

But the Wildcats had two things working in their favor. That 1985 season was the last before a shot clock was added to the game. Massimino wisely worked it to his advantage. He strategized Villanova's stall-ball victories as well as the players executed it. Villanova eventually would win its title averaging just 55 points per game.

Massimino also strummed the underdog violin relentlessly. Angered that his team earned only an eighth seed and incensed that the Wildcats were assigned a first-round game against Dayton at Dayton, he decided early on that he would feed his players daily doses of us-against-them medicine. They downed every one.

"I'm sure the coaches will tell you it took us four years, but we finally started listening," Pinckney said. "There's some truth to that. We learned how to lead and bring everyone together. We learned late, unfortunately, but we learned."

Villanova survived the Flyers by two, upset top-seeded Michigan to reach the Sweet 16, got past No. 5 Maryland there, and undid second-seeded North Carolina to stun the basketball world and reach Lexington, Kentucky, site of the Final Four.

Riding their magic carpet even further, the Wildcats topped Memphis 52–45 to reach the national championship game. On the other side of the bracket sat Georgetown, which had all but rolled through the tourney field to its seemingly predestined title, beating teams by an average of 15.6 points per game.

Understandably the Wildcats were given little chance to win the game, Georgetown deemed nine-point favorites to win it all. To win, most people believed, Villanova would have to play flawlessly.

Today, that April 1 game is still referred to as The Perfect Game.

Villanova shot 22-of-28 from the floor (78.6 percent) and connected on 22-of-27 of its free throws, pulling off a victory perhaps more improbable than any in NCAA history. The Wildcats, in fact, remain the lowest-seeded team to win a title.

That championship marked a high-water mark not only for Villanova as a program, but for Catholic schools everywhere.

No one could foretell it then but change—big change—was on the horizon for college basketball.

"The last Catholic school to make the Final Four before Villanova was Villanova in 2009," Jerardi said. "The last Catholic school to win before Villanova was Villanova in 1985. The reality is, the power conferences have all the advantages."

A reality which made the 2016 Villanova team, if not a Cinderella, a long shot.

Jerardi's numbers only begin to explain just how unlikely it's become for a team like Villanova to win a title. Consider: from 1947 to 1985, eight of the 39 national championships won belonged to Catholic universities—Holy Cross in 1947, La Salle in 1954, San Francisco in 1955 and 1956, Loyola (Illinois) in 1963, Marquette in 1977, Georgetown in 1984, and Villanova. And in 1985, Catholic schools claimed three of the four national semifinal spots. In the 31 years since, a Catholic school has only made it to the Final Four six times—Providence in 1987, Seton Hall in 1989, Marquette in 2003, Georgetown in 2007, and Villanova in 2009 and 2016.

What caused the seismic shift? Money, of course. The deeper-pocketed state schools, with bigger alumni bases and coffers already lined with football money, started to pay attention to basketball. Recognizing the burgeoning interest in their sport that the expanded tourney field brought in 1985, the NCAA and CBS in 1991 signed a seven-year deal worth $1 billion. With each conference divvying up its share of that money to its members, basketball suddenly became a lot more attractive, and a lot more lucrative, to everyone.

"It comes down to resources," former Villanova athletic director Vince Nicastro told the *Philadelphia Daily News* in 2005. "Since the mid-'80s, there's been a shift in the power. Some of those schools were pure football schools and, all of a sudden, they said, 'We could do this in basketball,' and they started to invest in basketball."

Investment equated to brand-new practice facilities, chartered flights to and from games, nutritionists on staff, and arena renovations or, in some places, complete rebuilds. The bigger schools simply had more money to spend. That holds true to this day. According to the U.S. Department of Education's Equity in Athletics data, Villanova basketball produced $10 million in revenues and the entire athletic department generated $37 million. By comparison North Carolina, its title game foe, amassed $20 million in basketball revenue alone, and $85 million overall.

Squeezed by the competition and without the money that football can generate, Catholic schools faced an uncertain future, viewed more as nice little throwbacks to what was, as opposed to an integral part of what college basketball could be.

"The structure has just changed so much," former Seton Hall coach P.J. Carlesimo told the *Philadelphia Daily News* in 2005. "It can still happen, but it's just a function of the numbers. In the old days, it just wasn't like that. There just wasn't a hierarchy. The way kids perceive where to go now is just so night-and-day different."

And then the sport threw another wicked curveball into the mix. Burned by too many high school graduates turning pro unprepared for the rigors of basketball and an adult lifestyle, the NBA instituted an age limit prior to the 2006 draft. In order to be eligible to enter the NBA, players must be 19 years old and one year removed from their high school graduation. By changing its rule, the NBA drastically altered the face of college basketball.

The same sport that once held freshmen out of competition—the great Bill Walton was not eligible to play in his first season at UCLA— became the youngest man's game.

The so-called one-and-done rule turned college basketball into a layover, a part-time residence for athletes who otherwise would be pros. It also further fanned the flames of the already fiercely competitive recruiting wars, with coaches vying for the attention of a handful of would-be ringers who could change their programs' fate, even if only for a season. The winners of the coveted talent trended toward the programs who offered the most exposure, the best facilities and staffs to train with, and the programs whose track records already were well established.

In the last 10 years, 96 freshmen have left after their first year of college. Of the 96, only seven came from teams outside of what were considered power conferences at the time of the draft—Shawne Williams of Memphis in 2006, Derrick Rose of Memphis in 2008, Tyreke Evans of Memphis in 2009, Hassan Whiteside of Marshall in

2010, Anthony Bennett of UNLV in 2013, Rashad Vaughn of UNLV in 2015, and Henry Ellenson of Marquette in 2016. (It's worth noting that from 2006 through 2009, Memphis was considered a basketball elite despite its Conference USA league affiliation, appearing in the Elite Eight in 2006, the national championship game in 2008, and the Sweet 16 in 2009.) Conventional wisdom long has held that he who amasses the most talent wins. The teams that lured the most future pro players—those good enough to leave early—naturally seemed more fast-tracked for quick success.

That one-two punch of dollars and draftees, then, conspired to make Villanova an anomaly and, yes, a long shot.

"I think in the current climate, you're forced to ask yourself, how are we going to survive?" Raftery said.

Villanova searched for its own answer.

Though school administrators and athletic leaders both understood Villanova was a financial underdog and not the same as a state school, they refused to accept that equated to second rate. In fact, the university at one point underwent a strategic planning and branding exercise, designed to see what people thought of it. When the consultants went so far as to suggest the school, and not just the basketball program, was a little engine that could, university administrators bristled. All these years later, despite growing its basketball program and stretching its wings as a nationally ranked institution, people still suggested it was 1985.

"We may be smaller," Nicastro said. "But in a lot of ways, we are big-time contenders. So it's a nice narrative to have, but I don't think it's entirely true."

Instead Villanova has carved its niche as special but not entirely different. The Wildcats cannot match the likes of North Carolina dollar for dollar, but as the flagship sport on the campus, the basketball program also does not have to compete with—or lose out to—football for money or attention. Its overall budget, while small compared to bigger schools, is easily the biggest among the university sports. The basketball team's expenses are $8.1 million; football, the next closest sport, spends $6.6 million.

Like the big schools, the Wildcats charter to and from every game. They, too, have a nutritionist on staff and a strength coach assigned to their team. Spearheaded by Wright, who was heavily involved in the planning and fund-raising, they also have a practice facility—the Davis Center—that includes a practice court, locker room, weight room, cinema room, and office space.

It's when you travel up to the third floor of that building that you discover what makes Villanova a little different. Treadmills, free weights, and other fitness equipment fill the space, to be used by the entire Villanova campus community. The Davis Center houses their fitness facility, too. A student traveling up the stairs to use the tread-mill will regularly bump into the national championship–winning coach on his way down from his second-floor office.

That doesn't happen at Duke.

"Nova is a unique place," former assistant Billy Lange said with a chuckle.

But stretching a dollar is one thing; stretching a roster is another. In the history of the program only six Villanova players have left college early for the NBA, and since the advent of the one-and-done rule, not a single freshman has bolted after his first year. Since 2010, Villanova has not landed a recruiting class ranked in the top 25. In fact, the four classes that made up the 2016 roster never earned much respect from recruiting gurus at all. Kris Jenkins, Josh Hart, and Darryl Reynolds together rated 31st in the country; Phil Booth and Mikal Bridges were ranked 37th; Ryan Arcidiacono and Daniel Ochefu together didn't even crack the top 60.

The Wildcats were viewed as very good college players, which is to say not necessarily future NBA stars. They were, in fact, so interchangeable and similarly skilled it was impossible to pinpoint who the star of the team was. The closest Villanova could come to a Buddy Hield of Oklahoma or a Marcus Paige of North Carolina was Arcidiacono, and half the television announcers still struggled to pronounce his name properly.

"We're not sexy," Wright said. "I get that."

The coach, however, would not concede that made his roster somehow inferior. He bristled when people called the Wildcats throw-backs, as if to imply their old-school dedication would not fit in the present-day world. He half-jokingly called them "enlightened," arguing that they had professional basketball aspirations like anyone else but weren't in a race to get there. He held onto the value of four-year players, even while the rest of the world had mad crushes on freshmen, and insisted that players who worked together for a common good could be as good as any collection of individuals.

"We're an all-excess kind of people—four-star and eight-star, we fall in love with the prognostications," Raftery said. "Jay decided he wasn't going to sell his soul because this kid is the best ever."

To a large extent, Wright's was a conscious decision, a direct result of an unsuccessful trip down the other rabbit hole after the 2009 Final Four. He had tried the other way, the seemingly more direct route to success, and didn't care for it.

"When I was there, I remember we were always pushing to get this guy on the list," Pinckney said. "It was, 'Hey, we gotta get this guy because all of the top teams are interested.' You get into that rat race. Those other schools, there's such a history of having the No. 1 class or

No. 2, and then from that, you have to have the No. 1 or No. 2 draft pick. It all gets tied together and it's really hard to get out of."

But in truth it was also borne out of a good dose of pragmatism. A few years back, Lange and Jason Donnelly, then the director of basketball operations, purposefully took a hard look at recruiting. Studying lists of top-ranked high school players and their college choices, they separated players into groups. The results weren't surprising—a handful of schools landed the large majority of the best players. There was an unmistakable hierarchy in college hoops. Of those 96 one-and-done players, nearly half went to the same six schools—Kentucky, Duke, Kansas, UCLA, Ohio State, and Texas.

Lange and Donnelly rightly concluded that there was no point in trying to beat other schools at a game you could never even play.

"We're not in that upper tier, and we're just not going to beat those schools out for guys. So how do you beat them?" Lange said. "Well we decided you figure out how to beat them from October through March as opposed to trying to beat them in July and September."

But could that method actually work? Could a team turn conventional wisdom on its ear and not just win, but win big, without big money and without courting the single best players in the country?

Villanova 77, North Carolina 74, offered an emphatic yes.

A year after Duke won a title and immediately said good-bye to three of its freshmen stars, the same year that John Calipari brazenly declared that all of his eligible Kentucky players would consider the NBA draft (including three freshmen who eventually would be drafted), Villanova won a national championship in April and two months later, did not have a single player drafted. It marked the first time since 1997 that a team won a title without any of its players selected in the ensuing draft. Even that plucky 1985 team, for all its underdog status, sent two players directly to the NBA—Pinckney was selected 10th overall and McClain was picked up in the second round.

"It furthers the mindset that a college program can win with the right guys instead of just the best NBA prospects," said veteran sportswriter Pat Forde of Yahoo!Sports. "There is a formula that can be tapped into, with the right mix of veterans who are good players and team-oriented and well coached. I would say the surest route to a championship remains overwhelming talent, but it doesn't have to be that way. Villanova reinforced that."

Villanova's way isn't the easiest route to success, to be sure. It's a lot easier to collect the top talent, manage egos and playing time, and roll a ball out onto the court. But as more and more schools understand what Lange and Donnelly figured out—the best players are generally going to choose a handful of colleges—Villanova has proven there is an alternative method.

And that's a very popular message with everyday people.

"The Wildcats weren't a team driven by egos or coddled youth," said ESPN.com basketball reporter Andy Katz. "This was a team built on the backs of four-year players and rotation players who came together for a common goal."

It's an even more popular route with college coaches. There are 351 schools playing Division I basketball. Most resemble Villanova more than Kentucky, Kansas, or Duke.

"You don't have to sell this dream of kids playing in the sandlot, staying together for four years to get you a once-in-a-lifetime moment," said Xavier coach Chris Mack. "If you get really good players and they're committed to one another, you can win it all. Villanova proved that."

The Wildcats also upended the notion that, in order to achieve individual goals, an athlete should only think of himself.

Arcidiacono, a suburban Philadelphia kid who isn't quick enough by NBA standards, and Ochefu, a tweener, both signed free-agent contracts after college. Arcidiacono is with the San Antonio Spurs and Ochefu with the Washington Wizards.

"You can always integrate someone on your team that has a championship mentality," said Pinckney, who has worked in the NBA as an assistant coach. "You can have a championship mentality and not win, but then you have to prove it. They've already proven it. They walk through the door and their calling card says, 'I'm a champion.'"

After the confetti and streamers, enough to cover the court like a celebratory paper snowstorm, finally stopped falling, the champions gathered on a makeshift stage at NRG Stadium. They wore their brand-new hats and T-shirts, declaring Villanova as the national champions. The gear wasn't necessary. The grins on their faces gave it away.

Since 1987, Luther Vandross' "One Shining Moment" has served as the national championship coda, the closing notes to the college basketball season. A collection of the best, craziest, and most emotional moments of the NCAA Tournament, the montage tugs at everyone's still raw emotions, especially the last team standing, the only one of those 351 Division I programs able to watch it live on the championship floor.

Yet as the Wildcats gathered, they were surprisingly calm—maybe not Jay Wright calm, but at least subdued. Their arms wrapped around one another's shoulders, they stared up at the big screen and watched the video, walk-ons and starters all mixed together as they have been all season. Henry Lowe, Patrick Ferrell, and Kevin Rafferty didn't play in the title game, but they were considered an integral part of the team, their contributions to the senior class as valued as those made by Arcidiacono and Ochefu.

And so there they stood, smiles from cheek to cheek and eyes wide as saucers, Arcidiacono sandwiched between Booth and Ferrell, Hart leaning forward, his elbows resting on the railing. Just a little behind them and off to the right stood Jenkins, holding the championship trophy in front of him. He had no intention, he said later, of letting it go. He might have been the least emotional of all, or perhaps more accurately the most dazed. His teammates cheered and patted him on his new championship hat as the video showed his shot going in, but Jenkins barely allowed himself a smirk. At first he nodded his head, as if to say he knew all along what would happen, but when the video ended he couldn't help himself. His nod changed to a shake.

Weeks later Jenkins was still somewhere between the two. He understood why Villanova had accomplished what it had accomplished and yet at the same time, couldn't quite comprehend it.

"We got better every part of this season, right down to the last 4.7 seconds," he said. "It's weird because at that time, it was the biggest moment for all of us, of all of our basketball careers, and for us to stay cool, to stay calm, in the moment, it's crazy. But it's also who we are."

In so many ways, really, this Villanova team had been preparing for this moment for years. Maybe not a buzzer-beating game winner in the national title game exactly, but a moment that embodied who they were. Unlike the 1985 team, a merry band of underdogs who came out of nowhere to win a championship, these Wildcats never wavered in their belief in themselves. Others might have looked at Villanova's finances, roster, and past NCAA flops and not seen a formula for the highest form of success.

The players believed people weren't looking at the picture properly.

Money doesn't win basketball games any more than recruiting rankings win basketball games. People do.

"Every coach does the same thing. We watch guys and we're always looking for the best player," Jones said. "Who's the best? Who's playing the best? Of course that matters but not enough time is spent on who are the best people. There's got to be a place for that, too. These guys were really talented but they wanted to be part of something bigger than themselves. That's why they won."

And strangely they won because, somewhere between a 2010 second-round-loss to Saint Mary's and a second-round loss to N.C. State in 2015, Villanova stopped defining itself by the final score.

That really is why Wright reacted the way he did.

For many people, even Wright's explanations—that he was talking to himself, that coaches always are worried about the next play—though believable enough, somehow rang a little hollow, too pat an answer for a reaction so utterly inexplicable.

But removed from the mayhem and able to exhale, Wright finally got to the heart of his near flatline response. For four years he'd been telling his players to let the results go, to dig deeper to measure their own value and appreciate the totality of the journey, not the finality of the finish.

How could Wright possibly change now?

"If you're going to say during the failures that we're not going to judge ourselves by what we do in the tournament, we can't say now we're the greatest thing in the world," he said. "This happened because it was never our goal. Our goal wasn't to win a national championship. It was to be the best team we could be by the end. With this group, things fell into place that when they became the best team they could be, it happened to be the national championship. So we're going to enjoy the hell out of this. But to us, this team is no more special than any of the teams that superseded them just because they won it all."

Bang.

She didn't say it, didn't even mouth the word like Jay Wright. But in her head? Yes, in her head Val Ackerman thought the same thing as Wright.

"Bang!"

In the opinion of the Big East commissioner, her league did not need to be vindicated or legitimized. She also knew that she was of the minority opinion. Most people, in fact, had been reserving judgment on her conference, unsure where it fit in the new world order of college sports, and in need of a little proof.

"This game was a test—a bit of a test—for our league," Ackerman said. "And we passed."

At one time, no one would have asked the Big East to prove its worth. At the height of its game, the league boasted one of the most formidable membership lineups in college basketball history. Five Hall of Fame coaches have stalked its sidelines. Seven of its member schools owned national championships. Its history was filled with memorable moments, from Georgetown coach John Thompson declaring Manley Field House closed, to the six-overtime Big East Tournament marathon game between Connecticut and Syracuse. A force in the national picture, the league long has gobbled up NCAA bids, including a record 11 teams in 2011.

But in 2016, this Big East was not that Big East. Reconstructed amid conference realignment, this Big East needed a defining moment. Kris Jenkins and Villanova provided it.

When NCAA president Mark Emmert passed the championship trophy to Wright and Villanova, the exchange was as significant for Butler, Creighton, DePaul, Georgetown, Marquette, Providence, Seton Hall, St. John's, and Xavier as it was for the Wildcats. A "halo effect," Ackerman called it, the entire league enveloped by Villanova's success.

Understandably the league boss didn't want the moment to end. Ackerman lingered at NRG Stadium long after everyone had cleared the floor, staying until nearly 2:00 in the morning. Moved by the sincere congratulations and warm embraces she received from colleagues, she simply wanted to take it all in, to not miss a second of a historic moment for her league. Ackerman also allowed herself a few minutes of reflection, to retrace the new Big East's journey from daring upstart to national champion.

A Big 12 team has not won a national championship since 2008. The Big Ten's drought stretches back to 2000 and the Pac 12's even longer, at 19 years. Yet in three short years of existence, the Big East, a league many thought couldn't survive, stood atop college basketball.

"It was exhilarating, but I was also drained, just emotionally drained," Ackerman said. "The weight had been lifted. What else is there to prove? Winning the national championship is the Holy Grail and we did it."

That the very notion of Villanova and the Big East winning a title had gone from entirely plausible to highly improbable in just a handful of years says everything about how drastically things have changed in college sports. College basketball always has been the Everyman game. The all-inclusive NCAA Tournament gives every team a chance to win a national title and the Cinderella moments that give the tournament its allure allows every team to dream big. When Ole Miss loses to Memphis in football, it's called an upset. When Bryce Drew converts an improbable hook-and-ladder to lift Valparaiso over the Rebels, it's called March Madness.

Of course, budgetary constraints create a hierarchy of the likely victors versus the unlikely, but Butler, George Mason, and Virginia Commonwealth, all Final Four participants, remind everyone that unlikely can happen.

With the advent of the Bowl Championship Series, everything has changed. With its escalating television demands, football has all but hijacked college sports. In attempts—often increasingly desperate ones—to align themselves with teams and conferences that are more financially attractive, university presidents have chucked tradition and history to the wind, quite literally rearranging college athletics to the point that it is almost unrecognizable. Old rivalries have died, killing geographic logic right along with them.

The Pac 12 (as in Pacific Ocean), for example, now includes land-locked Colorado and Utah. Maryland, a charter member of the Atlantic Coast Conference, turned away from its roots to join the Big Ten. Missouri ended a more than 100-year-old Border War rivalry with Kansas when it bolted the Big 12 for the SEC, while West Virginia opted to join the Big 12, despite the fact that the closest member school sits nearly 900 miles away.

Ultimately conference realignment turned downright cannibalistic, with bigger leagues feeding off the smaller and weaker ones. Those with little in the way of football history and less in the form of good football programs were especially vulnerable. That left the Big East ripe for picking.

In truth, the conference long had been a case study in the mess of realignment. Founded on the backbone of basketball, it had grudgingly turned to football to secure its survival in the modern world. In doing so, it killed its very core.

For more than 20 years, the league stayed largely the same, grouped together as Dave Gavitt intended with like-minded, Eastern-seaboard-hugging, basketball-centric schools. College athletics stayed virtually the same as well. Through 1990, no league had more than 10 members and none had divided itself into divisions. Football didn't crown league champions through title games, either.

But in 1991, recognizing that football was starting to gain traction, then Big East commissioner Mike Tranghese welcomed Rutgers, Miami, West Virginia, Virginia Tech, and Temple to the fold, allowing the league to field a football-playing division. It was the first move in what would launch more than a decade of chaos and turmoil within the Big East and around the country. A year later the Southeastern Conference expanded to 12 teams and added a conference championship game, and in 1994 Penn State joined the Big Ten.

The race, essentially was on.

In 2003, Big East charter member Boston College, plus Virginia Tech and Miami, left the league for the ACC. In response, the Big East added Cincinnati, Louisville, South Florida, DePaul, and Marquette, swelling into a mammoth 16-team league that, while successful, always felt like a jigsaw puzzle that didn't have the right pieces. Some members were big state schools, others small and private. Some identified with football success, others relied on basketball for branding. Divergent needs created divergent interests. As the need to capitalize on football success overtook college athletics, the Big East felt the push/pull perhaps more than any league.

"As it was described to me, there was tension in the old conference," said Ackerman, who wasn't the commissioner at the time. "It was in terms of what the football schools needed in terms of competing with others and what it meant in terms of configuration."

Tranghese, only the second commissioner in the league's history, announced his retirement in 2008 and John Marinatto, a company man who had grown up in the conference, was announced as his replacement. Though well versed in Big East history, Marinatto was not necessarily as equipped as his predecessor to stand toe to toe with the college athletics power brokers who ruled the day. The others were lawyers, men who had grown in stature as their leagues had asserted their strength. Marinatto came up as a sports information director at Providence. His devotion to the league was deep but he was not the shrewd businessman the Big East needed. When Big Ten commissioner Jim Delany said in 2009 that his league would examine expansion, the Big East's days essentially were numbered.

With Delany's announcement—followed shortly by a similar proclamation from Larry Scott at the Pac 12—the hunt and jockeying was officially on. Colorado was the first to leap, moving from the Big 12 to the Pac 12 on June, 20, 2010, creating the first crack in college athletics' fault line. A mere 14 months later Nebraska left for the Big Ten, Texas A&M for the SEC, and schools everywhere were rumored to be moving anywhere.

Behind the scenes in April 2011, Big East presidents were presented with a nine-year, $1.4 billion deal with ESPN. But eyeing up a recent $250 million per season package the Pac 12 negotiated, the presidents voted unanimously to turn down ESPN's offer.

"I think that was the stupidest decision ever made in college athletics," an anonymous source later told CBSSports.com.

The decision would, in fact, be the league's undoing. Five months later Pittsburgh and Syracuse, sensing that their league was falling apart, stunned fans, media, and college sports folks everywhere when they announced they would leave the Big East for the ACC.

Losing Pitt hurt. Losing Syracuse was a body blow. A charter member of the conference, the central New York school had long factored into the history of the league. Some of the Big East's biggest stars came from Syracuse; some of the conference's most unforgettable moments included the Orange. The school and conference were practically synonymous with one another.

"None of it bothered me until Syracuse left," former Georgetown coach John Thompson said in 2013. "When Syracuse left, I said, 'Et tu, Brute?' That got me. As much as I hated them in the competitive sense, I respected them, the fans, and what we had going on. When you heard that was going to fall apart, I said to myself, 'Those damn football people. They took our song and changed it.'"

Syracuse coach Jim Boeheim wasn't exactly thrilled with the decision, either. He bemoaned the thought of playing conference tournament games in Greensboro, North Carolina, instead of Madison Square Garden, jokingly wondering where he could find the same meals he'd grown accustomed to eating in New York. But the Hall of Fame coach understood the business decision. Most people did. The ACC offered good basketball but more critical to the current climate, promised a more prosperous and more secure football future.

"At some point, there's hard feelings because you think you're partners with someone," said former Villanova athletic director Vince Nicastro. "But I think at the end of the day, people understood that if I were in their shoes, I probably would have done the same thing. So after the initial sting—the I can't believe that happened, how could they do that?—rational people would say, 'Ah, you know what? I probably would have done the same thing if I had the choice.'"

The Big East tried to salvage itself but made decisions that were desperate and haphazard, with seemingly little thought or concern as to the root of the conference's identity. The league added Texas

Christian temporarily, but then the Horned Frogs quickly reneged and bolted for the Big 12. The Big East then announced the additions of Houston, Boise State, Central Florida, SMU, Temple, East Carolina, Tulsa, Navy (in football only), and Memphis, all added to bolster the football side of things. But the conglomeration of schools—none other than Boise State a legit football presence, none other than Temple with much of a recent basketball history—only added to the ragtag look of the league, not to mention the laughably expanded geographic footprint.

When in the span of the 2011–12 calendar year, West Virginia (to the Big 12), Louisville (to the ACC), Rutgers (to the Big Ten), and Notre Dame (to the ACC for everything but football) left, what remained of the Big East more closely resembled an Ellis Island of college athletics rather than the once proud power it had been. Worse, the divide between football-playing schools and basketball schools was even wider, the two groups not only lacking in conformity but robbed of any traditional relationships. On the one side sat Houston, Central Florida, SMU, Temple, Memphis (after the last round of defections, Boise State switched gears, opting instead for the Mountain West), Cincinnati, Connecticut, Tulsa, East Carolina, and Navy; the other side of the table included DePaul, Georgetown, Villanova, Providence, Seton Hall, St. John's, and Marquette.

The league was, in simple terms, a mess.

"We wanted to stay connected to the football people because there was a value in that, but at some point, that value started to feel like it was eroding because we were going to be going all over the country," Nicastro said.

With everything in disarray the presidents of the basketball-playing schools—the Catholic 7, as they'd come to be known—started talking privately amongst themselves. Encouraged by Tranghese, the former commissioner, to make sure that they'd be protected if more drastic changes happened, they realized that although the league was in an identity crisis, the seven schools were not. They knew who they were, and more who they were not. None had big-time football and therefore, they weren't beholden to the chase for football money.

They were an aberration in modern college sports, yet also the biggest victims of realignment. Of all the recent decisions made by their conference, few had been done with their schools in mind. Everything had been generated in an effort to improve football. Basketball, their flagship sport, was towed along for the ride.

The Catholic 7 presidents finally realized if no one else was going to consider them first, it was up to them to make their schools a priority. Through private meetings, countless phone calls, and more than one gathering in New York, they solidified their allegiance to one another.

"We had been bystanders," Nicastro said. "We didn't have much control over what was going to happen. Schools would leave and then schools would come in and it was just happening to us. The presidents felt that, as a group, we needed to control our own destiny, whatever that destiny was going to be."

The Catholic 7 ultimately chose perhaps the most daring path of any carved in all of the conference realignment era: they effectively opted to secede. With no offices, no name, no commissioner, no schedule, no television deal, and above all, no football, they decided to create their own space in college athletics.

"The big question was, if you weren't attached to a football league, would that somehow mitigate the influence you had?" Nicastro said. "A lot of people thought it would."

Of course, it's worth pausing here to note that people once told Dave Gavitt his lark wouldn't work, either.

In July 1979, the Providence coach and athletic director decided to bring together a group of athletic administrators for a meeting on Cape Cod to present his plan.

"He wanted to create a league with like-minded schools in the East who wanted to play basketball," Tranghese said. "He didn't have a long-range plan. He said, 'This is what we're going to do, and we'll do it the best we can.'"

Not everyone loved the idea, including some big-name coaches whose opinions mattered.

"You're talking to one of those guys who wasn't in favor of the situation," legendary St. John's coach Lou Carnesecca said in 2013. "I thought we had a good situation."

Added Georgetown's Thompson: "I don't think coaches joined enthusiastically. I know I sure was skeptical."

But Gavitt was as beloved as he was respected, and though a dreamer, also rather tenacious. He convinced the naysayers and the skeptics that his idea would not only work, but that it would work so well that one day the still unnamed league would play in the biggest arena in the world, Madison Square Garden. After kicking around a bunch of names—the North Atlantic Alliance, the Colonial League, and, half-jokingly, the Mayflower Compact—they settled on a simple, yet logical choice—the Big East Conference.

And so in December 2012, some 20-plus years later, the Big East, a league built on a dream and a risk was essentially back where it started, ready to take another big leap of faith.

"Knowing what I know now, I do think it was something of an act of courage by these presidents to say, 'You know what? This is who we are. We don't fault the football schools but that's not us,'" Ackerman said. "To have the seven make the decision they did, to withdraw and have the vision they did, that was a very brave decision."

In many ways, the decision made in December 2012 was even riskier than the one Gavitt made in 1979. When Gavitt aligned the Big East schools he was capitalizing on the popularity of college basketball at a time when television contracts didn't exist and ESPN was in its infancy. Things were different, less complicated even, the financial chasm that would come to divide schools so dramatically only just beginning.

Gavitt, too, had fortuitous timing. The Big East was born in lockstep with ESPN, one needing exposure and the other programming. Theirs would be a marriage that would benefit both sides as both grew.

And just as the league was beginning, a kid by the name of Patrick Ewing was tearing up the high school basketball courts in Boston. Gavitt, a native New Englander, knew how special Ewing was, and when Ewing signed his letter of intent to play at Georgetown, Gavitt knew what it meant for his league.

"I saw Dave later that day and he said, 'It's time, Michael,'" Tranghese remembered. "'We're going to New York.'"

The Catholic 7's timing was considerably worse. The best players weren't going anywhere for long in the era of one-and-done players and most were opting for the big-name schools. Worse, the seven schools were banking on themselves and basketball's marketability at a time when football was cashing all of the checks. No one was clamoring for television contracts with basketball schools, and any agreement the schools might be able to make would be for considerably less, making fielding not just basketball teams but the other non-revenue sports a challenge.

The chasm between the two groups, the haves and have-nots, was so stark that those who had aligned themselves properly and successfully were deemed the Power 5 (the Pac 12, Big Ten, Big 12, SEC, and ACC) conferences. Theoretically, then, the others were powerless.

Certainly there was sense to the Catholic schools' thinking. After being fed a steady dose of new teams with little regard to their impact on basketball, their decisions would be theirs alone, no longer muddied by the burning questions of how they'd help football. "We're authentic," Wright later would say.

But could authentic work in a prefabricated world? How could a basketball-centric league survive in a football-dominated world?

"There was a strong sentiment that what we were doing made a lot of sense in a world that was making less sense at the time," Nicastro said. "The world was getting crazier by the day, and I think a lot of people in our business saw ours as being maybe more rational. But I know a lot of people also wondered whether or not it would work."

The soon-to-be league didn't have much time to figure it out. They formally announced they would leave and re-form in December 2012. By the following fall, they'd have to field teams. What followed, then, was a fortuitous, if chaotic, combination of hard work and good luck. The league temporarily hired former Big 12 commissioner Dan Beebe to help guide it through its exit strategy and rebirth, and leaned heavily on Neal Pilson, a onetime president of CBS Sports, to help negotiate the most important deal of all—a television package.

In a frenetic three months, it all somehow came together. Agreeing to take considerably less from the exit fees the old league had amassed over the years, the Catholic 7 schools were released from their old ties, allowed to keep the Big East name, and continue their basketball tournament in Madison Square Garden. Of even greater significance, with Pilson's help, the league brokered a deal with Fox Sports 1, a new network stem of Fox Sports that was prepping to launch in August. The 12-year deal was for a reported $500 million, far less than other football leagues were getting but a more than fair market price for the new basketball league.

The (new) Big East also announced it would add Butler, Xavier, and Creighton to it roster to form a 10-member league, and in June announced Ackerman as the commissioner.

"Part of it was, to be honest, not knowing better," Ackerman said of her decision. "I came from the outside, so I was less tuned in to the nuances of alignment, the pressures and challenges brought in by big-time football. It struck me a very much within the possibility, with the pillars that this conference had, these schools with basketball traditions, I thought we had what it took to be successful."

With the Humpty Dumpty league finally pieced back together, those in the Big East were excited but also understandably nervous. Change is always scary and this was a big one, especially for teams and schools who had essentially run under the same banner for almost 40 years.

"It was difficult in the sense that we were dealing with an unknown," said Villanova's associate head coach Baker Dunleavy. "The old Big East was something we'd always been associated with and it propped us up and made us relevant. Being associated with other programs like we were, that really benefited us. The new teams, we had great respect for them, but we didn't know them. How committed were they going to be with taking the next step?"

Certainly people were hopeful. In an era where so many decisions had been based on money and even greed, the Big East had staked a claim for the idealists who still believed that collegiality could exist in college athletics. Though borne out of necessity, the conference members were connected by more than just a need to generate money. The geography had stretched but essentially the league's principles were not that much different than the ones Gavitt used to form the Big East—a group of like-minded schools banding together to form a basketball-centric league.

Yes, the Big East lacked football profits, but the schools also were unencumbered by football's expenses.

"I said a long time ago, and I got pooh-poohed because people thought I was making excuses, but in the big leagues what's happening is the haves and have-nots, because the money is driven by football success," Tranghese said. "These schools didn't have that. They were all coming from essentially the same place."

Still the biggest, most basic question facing the Big East was would it thrive, instead of merely survive?

Its first hurdle, interestingly, was essentially getting over itself. To the Catholic 7 schools, keeping the Big East name was critical to maintaining the league's identity. The name conjured up the glory days, when the league ruled the day and its coaches and players were recognizable by one name—Rollie and Louie, P.J. and Big John, Mullins and Ewing and Pearl.

When, at the urging of university presidents, the Big East launched a brand review, it happily learned that many people attributed old league traits to the new conference.

"Urban, gritty, tough-nosed physical play—people did see the Big East as having a certain identity and it was linked to what the old Big East had achieved," Ackerman said.

Yet as positive as those perceptions were, as critical as the league's name was to keeping its history intact and securing its future, it also encouraged inevitable comparisons. *This* Big East was never going to be *that* Big East. In their defense, league administrators and coaches never tried to pretend that they were. When pressed to explain how they'd live up to their own name, they all sounded the same refrain— we're not trying to. Instead they asked for patience, to be given the proper amount of time for the conference to forge an identity that was linked to the past but not beholden to it.

"Every coach in this room understands their responsibility," Georgetown coach John Thompson III said in 2014. "That's obvious. But it takes time for history to be made."

Time and patience, however, are in short supply these days, especially in sports where coaches go from hot hire to hot seat practically overnight. Rather than celebrate and applaud the league for directing its own future, people were more interested in ruing the loss of the Big East's past. Once the conference was home to a who's who of coaches. Reporters annually attending media day would have to figure out how to split their time. To sit and listen to Jim Calhoun pontificate might mean missing some really interesting nuggets from Rick Pitino or entertaining banter from Jim Boeheim. Now Wright, who in the old regime was still the new kid on the block, was the longest-tenured coach.

Where once the strength of the league was understood and teams were justly rewarded with postseason berths based on the rigors of conference play, now people struggled to calculate the value of league wins. Was winning at Creighton as difficult as winning at Syracuse? Did beating Marquette carry the same merit as topping Louisville?

In its last year in the old configuration, eight league teams earned bids and one, Louisville, won the national championship. In its first year in its new version, four squads earned bids but all failed to survive the first weekend. Rubbing salt in the wound, old Big East member Connecticut won the national championship.

"People outside almost took the current Big East for granted," Tranghese said. "It's not the old Big East, so therefore it wasn't any good. I kept telling people, 'Forget what was. It doesn't exist anymore.

This is the new league and it just so happens to have the same name.' But that's hard for people to do."

And it's not like the skepticism was without merit. As Dick Jerardi, the *Daily News* columnist, pointed out, the schools that were saying they could compete were years removed from anything more than sporadic, fitful success. The history of the Big East included Georgetown and Villanova, St. John's and Providence. The more recent success of the league, though, belonged to teams such as Louisville and Syracuse, UConn and West Virginia. The new Big East had founded itself on a nostalgic ideal but what if that ideal was outdated?

After all, DePaul and St. John's were decades removed from their glory years. In 2013, DePaul was on its fourth head coach in 10 years (and two years later would make yet another change) while St. John's was still trying to recapture the magic it enjoyed under Carnesecca. The beloved Louie spent 19 years at the school; in the 19 years since he left, seven coaches had tried to fill his shoes. Seton Hall's progress had stalled since Carlesimo's days and Providence was only just starting to reassert itself after years of decay. Even once-proud Georgetown had lost some of its luster, unable to make even a regional semifinal since 2007.

"We have to prove ourselves," Wright said at the league's onset. "Not because we're not a good league, but just because we're new."

The team best positioned to deliver that proof was Villanova. The Wildcats were not only the most recent Final Four participant, but also the most consistent performer over the last decade. The guy who was the new kid on the block in the old regime now not only was the wise leader, his team was expected to carry the Big East flag.

And for much of the regular season they did, winning games, climbing up the rankings, and giving the Big East a presence in the national picture. But then came March, and if a team is judged by its NCAA finish, certainly a conference is by extension. Those early round losses that haunted Villanova dogged the Big East, too, as it tried to earn its credibility.

At the end of the 2013–14 season, the league's first, four teams were rewarded with NCAA Tournament bids, but only Creighton, with player of the year Doug McDermott, and Villanova were awarded with single-digit seeds.

On the first day of the tournament, Xavier, seeded 12th, lost in the First Four to N.C. State. Two days later, 11th-seeded Providence exited, dismissed by North Carolina. Creighton and Villanova each won their first-round games but before the weekend was over, both were sent home; the Wildcats, the No. 2 seed, done in by UConn on Saturday, No. 3 Creighton crushed by 30 points by Baylor on Sunday.

The next season, the league already was earning its stripes. It not only earned six NCAA bids, of those six teams five were awarded seeds that positioned them as first-round favorites. St. John's, the sixth team, was in the most evenly matched first-round spot, a No. 9 seed to No. 8 San Diego State. The Red Storm would lose to the Aztecs and Providence would be upset by Dayton, but the four others advanced to the second day of the tourney. The good news ended quickly. Though Xavier would take the Big East to its first Sweet 16, topping would-be Cinderella Georgia State, Georgetown lost to Utah, Butler to Notre Dame, and most devastating of all, top-seeded Villanova failed to advance, done in by N.C. State.

"That certainly didn't silence the critics; it made them even louder," Xavier coach Chris Mack said. "It was really disappointing because I knew how good Villanova was. The NCAA Tournament is such a crapshoot with matchups. You have one bad shooting night and you're done, and that's what happened to Villanova. It diminished what everybody in the league knew—how tremendously hard they played, how together that team was. That's who that team was and it didn't resonate because they lost to a fledgling N.C. State team."

"We definitely let down the Big East," Wright said a year later. "We were a good enough team to advance and we didn't do it. We take responsibility for that and we take that responsibility seriously."

It was an onus that weighed heavily on Wright. He reiterated the sentiment privately to friends and coaches, and semi-privately in the summertime meetings with other Big East coaches. As a kid reared on the old league, he valued the relationships that served as the epicenter for the new league. He could have sought out a new job. Plenty speculated that he might, exchanging the unknown future in his new league for the more solid footing of an established conference. He never so much as toyed with leaving. Wright considers himself a Northeast guy first and a Big East guy second, and rather than flirt with other schools, he rolled up his sleeves to work on the new league.

"He was a valuable commodity as a coach, so you're always worried," Nicastro said of the concern that his coach might leave. "But he was so engaged in making this work."

Wright knew the best way to make the league work was for the teams to win, and without being arrogant knew his team was best suited to win those big games.

And twice Villanova had blown it.

From her New York office, Ackerman was well aware of the conference guilt Wright carried. New to college basketball herself, she leaned heavily on the more established Wright to deliver the league's message. He did so sincerely and effortlessly, holding true to the Big East's past while sounding the drum for the promise of the future, and Ackerman was rightly indebted to him for it.

She also understood why, in Wright's mind, his team's failures then reflected poorly on the entire conference. She, however, had a different opinion of things. Ackerman essentially believed in the message that Wright long had been selling to his players—that one NCAA loss did not negate all the positive Villanova had done for the Big East.

"I could feel his pain, but we never thought of it that way," Ackerman said. "It was never our conference view. It's too much of a burden for any one school to shoulder. Villanova had done everything we needed them to do and at some point, that's just the way the cookie crumbles. At the end of the year, there's only one happy school."

As much as Ackerman meant what she said, she did admit, albeit sheepishly, that when the buzzer sounded on the 2016 season and the one happy school was a Big East school, it was hard not to believe that her entire league had won.

"Sigh of relief," she said. "A definite sigh of relief."

Typically national championships are about the teams that win it. Conferences benefit financially, of course, and bask in the edges of their member team's glory. But in most cases, little mind is paid to what a title by one team does by extension for an entire conference. When Duke won its title in 2015, for example, it wasn't viewed as a shot in the arm for the ACC.

Then again, the ACC doesn't need a shot in the arm. The Big East did. Just as Villanova's losses once negatively impacted the league, the national title raised the entirety of the league in ways both small and big. Mack said that recruits who otherwise might not have been interested in Xavier are returning his calls more frequently. It's estimated that Kris Jenkins' buzzer beater will equate to $19.1 million for the league teams from the CBS television deal with the NCAA.

But it's in the broader spectrum that this title will resonate the most. The questions that so many people asked when the Catholic 7 presidents decided to go on their own now have answers.

Are leagues outside the Power 5 as talented as the rest? Yes.

Can teams without football money compete at the highest level? Yes.

And above all else, can a conference that doesn't fit the traditional mold not merely coexist but succeed? Yes.

"This was a statement that these kids play for real," Raftery said. "They're good and they're going to be a factor. College basketball isn't going to just be about the Power 5 and this league won't be an afterthought."

College athletics isn't done changing, not by a long shot. The Power 5 schools' stranglehold is increasing, not lessening. The NCAA has granted those conferences some measure of autonomy, allowing them to create rules and opportunities separate from their Division I counterparts. Their first venture, cost of attendance—essentially permitting schools to make up the financial difference between the value of a full scholarship and what it costs for an athlete to attend college— is threatening to further divide schools, turning the ones that can pay full cost of attendance into far more attractive destinations than those that cannot.

The Big East presidents have committed to full cost of attendance for all of their athletes, allowing the league to remain competitive, but it is certainly a burden for schools that simply don't have as much money in the budget. And there is no guarantee that is the final big change coming to college sports. Odds are it's just the tip of the iceberg. Doomsayers even foresee a day when the Power 5 schools essentially break off from everyone else to form their own competitive alliance. That could effectively kill the NCAA Tournament.

Nothing is certain, but then again nothing is out of the question, either. Going forward, then, it's even more critical that those programs that are the most vulnerable position themselves as future players in the cutthroat game of college athletics. That, in essence, is why Villanova's title was so critical for the Big East. En route to that championship, the Wildcats dismissed a Big Ten school (Iowa), an ACC school (Miami), two Big 12 schools (Kansas and Oklahoma), and then another ACC school, and arguably one of the most iconic programs in history, in North Carolina.

"I would hope this has quieted the naysayers and has proven that the Big East is real, that Villanova is real," Ackerman said.

Then she paused. She knows that one title isn't enough, that one team isn't enough, either.

"Ultimately our success will be measured by the depth of our success," she said. "One or two teams at the top every year, that's just not enough."

Back in 1979, Raftery was the head coach at Seton Hall, finishing up his run of stalking the sidelines before trading in his clipboard for a legendary broadcasting career. Raftery was popular among his Big East coaching brethren. He joked it was because everyone else could beat him and the Pirates but really, his good nature and jokester personality were the perfect antidote to a group with larger-than-life personalities and equally outsized egos. The Big East meetings, Raftery recalled, were unforgettable, the coaches trading four-letter words and insults as they tried to assert themselves in the pecking order, with the ever popular Gavitt keeping everyone in check.

Those personalities were the league's draw for the first few years. Still trying to figure itself out, moving the tournament from Providence to Syracuse to Hartford in its first three years, the Big East was more a curiosity than a commodity early on. In those years, the league fared well but essentially was carried by the core four—Syracuse, Georgetown, St. John's, and Villanova. They were the big names and the big winners, with Georgetown ascending to the top with its 1984 national championship.

And then came the breakout year, 1985, when the Hoyas owned the regular season, the league took over the Final Four by claiming three of the four spots, and Villanova won its storybook championship. Gavitt's pipe dream became a winning reality. Three years later, the league earned six bids, with Providence and Pittsburgh joining the rank and file. The conference never looked back again.

This is not 1985. So much has changed at Villanova, in college basketball, and in sports in general. But like that legendary championship, a title that vaulted a young league from the shadows into prominence, Villanova's title in 2016 has written the first chapter of the new Big East. It's up to the other teams to capitalize on what the Wildcats have started. But the opportunity, one that only three years ago many considered little more than a long shot, is there.

"This has been the gift that keeps on giving but success in this business is fleeting," Ackerman said. "You've always got something to prove because people forget, so we aren't done. Far from it. But I think in three years, we've proven a lot already."

The dogpile gave way to the trophy presentation, which led to "One Shining Moment" and finally to the press conference. The return to the team hotel, the Royal Sonesta, turned into a makeshift party. The players, many still in their uniforms, led the throngs of Villanova fans in a "Let's go, Nova!" chant before Jay Wright took the podium. Egging on the fans, he raised a paper with his written remarks and said, "I showed the guys, this is how confident I was in them. I had my speech written up before the game."

Later the team moved the party upstairs to a private room with family and close friends before finally shutting things down somewhere before dawn. The next day, after rounds of media—Kris Jenkins appeared on *Good Morning, America*—the team finally headed to the airport, boarding its charter flight home with a most-treasured piece of carry-on luggage, a national championship trophy.

Despite the endless party, despite the pieces of net stuck in their national championship baseball caps and the T-shirts proclaiming them the winners, the enormity of it all didn't hit the Villanova basketball team until the Wildcats got home.

"I don't think it sunk in right away," Jenkins said.

Not until they saw the fire trucks, two of them facing each other, waiting. As soon as the Villanova plane turned off the tarmac and toward the gate, the trucks went to work, spraying a water arch over the plane, signaling the national champions were home.

As the players and staff exited the plane to a handful of fans and a host of television cameras, they boarded three buses to take them back to campus. Escorted by police on the ground and news helicopters overhead, the buses pulled onto Interstate 95 South at 6:00 PM, about the worst time you can head onto a Philadelphia-area highway. Rush hour in the city, like it is in so many metropolitan areas, can be a soul-crushing test of patience.

Only as the Villanova buses headed to the on ramps to merge onto the highway, there was no one on the road. Not just no traffic, not a single car. The highway was eerily empty. The city had closed all of the roads—I-95 and another busy thoroughfare known locally as the Blue Route—from the airport to campus, guaranteeing the Wildcats a clear shot back home.

"That's when I was like, 'Okay, this is for real,'" Daniel Ochefu said. "That was surreal. There was no one on the road with us, just people off to the side honking their horns. It was crazy."

What does it feel like to win a national championship? Only a select group of people know, and most struggle with a good explanation. "I can't even describe it," countless athletes have said when pressed to describe their emotions in the immediate minutes after winning. Instant adrenaline and euphoria carry the moment but a true appreciation of the accomplishment takes time to sink in. It takes getting out of the insular circle of the team to grasp the enormity of it all.

In the days and weeks and months after Villanova's plane landed in Philadelphia, the Wildcats finally came to understand just what they had done.

"To have people come up to you and tell you what that shot meant to them, your peers and people older than you, man, I can't explain it," Jenkins said. "It's humbling."

With classes canceled, Villanova returned to a campus still in the throes of joy. The fans who packed the Pavilion to watch the game spilled into the street as soon as Jenkins' shot went in, and by the next morning the place was still buzzing. Every street corner already sported placards advertising Villanova championship gear for sale and the place was clogged with fans of all ages. The school had planned a welcome back rally, scheduled to begin around 4:00 PM, but the Wildcats travel schedule got derailed and the team didn't land at the airport until nearly 6:00. That didn't seem to matter to the thousands of fans who camped inside the football stadium on the chilly afternoon. Some took to their phones and social media to track the Wildcats' travels and relayed the information to fellow fans.

Finally, when the rat-a-tat from the blades of news choppers neared, fans knew the party was about to begin.

"They're coming!" one little boy, wearing a championship T-shirt, shouted to his mother.

One longtime Philly reporter shook his head and laughed.

"These kids," he said, "will never have to buy another beer around here."

No doubt this was a party years in the making, a catharsis for a city longing to celebrate, for a university whose shining moment was tinged with the sepia-colored tones of the past, and a league hungry to assert its place in college sports. That the improbable championship came via an impossible shot only added to the lure that will long follow this 2016 Villanova national championship team.

Before they left for Houston, the Wildcats were kids, some not old enough to even drink the free beer. When they returned they were legends.

After parking in the lot behind the Pavilion, the Wildcats entered the stadium through a tunnel and walked down a pathway lined with fans, high-fiving and posing for selfies along the way. As the pep band blared the fight song, Ochefu hugged the trophy to his chest. Once everyone was on stage, he hoisted it high to share with the delighted crowd.

"Nova Nation, we love you!" Wright shouted. "And you are the 2016 national champions!"

Ochefu, Ryan Arcidiacono, and Josh Hart each addressed the crowd, sounding a familiar refrain to their coach, thanking fans for their year-long support. Wright took back the microphone and, once the pep band quieted, yelled to the crowd, "Just for the hell of it, let's do it. When I say, 'Nova,' you say, 'Nation!'"

And the fans shouted their response giddily.

Finally Wright turned his players around so their backs faced the crowd and asked the fans to smush together. He snapped a championship selfie and immediately posted it on Twitter. "Nova Nation you are the best," he added to the tagline.

The whole gathering lasted maybe 40 minutes but it was enough to temporarily satiate a fan base that had waited 31 long years to celebrate.

Afterward the players and Wright met briefly with the media, overcome and amazed with the celebration they'd just witnessed.

"I'm at a loss for words," Jenkins said. "I'm still in shock."

And this was only the beginning of a summer-long celebration, the warm-up act to bigger parties still to come.

Three days later Wright parted the blinds and peeked through the window of his office. In the parking lot behind the Pavilion, K-9 dogs were busy sniffing a convoy of buses. From somewhere off in the distance police sirens sounded.

"Here comes our motorcade," Wright said. "This is crazy."

In a few hours, the Wildcats would leave their suburban campus for downtown Philadelphia. The city was throwing the team a championship parade, closing five city blocks to celebrate its newest champions. Like Villanova graduates, Philadelphians were hungry for a sports winner. In a city that loves its teams to the point of distraction, their devotion had rarely been rewarded. Philadelphia ranks sixth in the nation with the most sports championships—17—but most is not the same as latest. Once spoiled by a glut of championship parades—in the span of 23 years, Philly teams won six championships—fans were desperate for a winner. The Phillies' 2008 World Series title was the first—and only—since the 76ers won the NBA championship in 1983.

But early on that Friday morning, Wright enjoyed a brief respite from the hubbub that had been and was still to come. The small reception area outside of the men's basketball offices was a beehive of activity. The managers carted catering trays filled with water from the kitchenette to the team's theater room. Helene Mercanti, Wright's longtime administrative assistant, tried to keep up with the ringing phones while Arleshia Davidson, Wright's special assistant, darted back and forth tying up loose ends. A table had been added next to the usual display case to house the new hardware—Wright's coach of the year trophy, Ryan Arcidiacono's most outstanding player award, and, of course, the national championship trophy—clogging the area as parents and players filed in for a pre-parade breakfast. It wasn't even 10:00 in the morning.

Tucked behind the double doors and down the hallway, Wright sat in the quiet of his office, alone for maybe the first time in days. His morning had been filled with more media obligations and soon he'd turn on his smile to face the fans. But for a few minutes there wasn't any noise, or people asking for anything, just him and his thoughts. He was reflective, so proud of what his team had accomplished but also curious, trying to figure out how it would all play out going forward. Would things change—for him, for his team, for his university? Wright desperately hoped they wouldn't. He loved Villanova for a lot of reasons but tantamount among them was the sanity the job allowed. He could escape to his Jersey Shore home in the summer and enjoy the beach relatively unmolested. He could tinker with his team during the non-conference season while most city fans were preoccupied with the Eagles.

He didn't want to lose that. Wright wanted what seemed like a pipedream—to win a national title and go back to being an ordinary guy. He already had reached out to fellow coaches, including Louisville's Rick Pitino, for advice in navigating his new normal.

"He told me he left Kentucky for the Celtics in part because he said, 'I didn't want to be a rock star. I wanted to be a coach,'" Wright said. "I know exactly what he means."

Whether Wright could rediscover normal remained to be seen. First, there were a lot more rock star days ahead.

Following the motorcade to Center City, Wright and his team hopped aboard double-decker buses for the ride from 20th and Market streets to Dillworth Plaza, just outside of Philadelphia's iconic City Hall building. No one was quite sure what to expect for this parade. This was a college team, not a pro squad, and though Villanova has a long history with the city, it resides six miles outside of the Philly limits.

Plus the weather—only 40 degrees—wasn't exactly cooperating.

"I'm not a Philly guy, but I've spent more time here than anywhere else, but I still think of it as a pro sports town," associate head coach Baker Dunleavy said. "We have our great Villanova fans and in March everyone drops in to support us. But every other day of the year, this is a pro sports town. I wasn't sure what it would be like, but wow."

Wow, indeed. Dunleavy needn't have worried.

Fans crowded the streets, in some places as many as 15 to 20 deep, to fete their national champions. City officials later estimated the giddy crowd at 60,000. With street vendors hawking Villanova wares, iPhones turned to record the festivities, and fans toting creative signs—some asked Arcidiacono to be a prom date, others suggested Wright for president, and one clever student declared, "If you see my teacher, tell her I have a doctor's appointment"—the buses snaked down the parade route.

But instead of peeling off after the team passed by, the people on the streets fell in behind the buses, walking on to the rally in front of City Hall. With the crowd growing bigger and bigger, it was hard not to think of another iconic Philadelphia moment, albeit a fictional one. As Rocky Balboa jogged through his usual route preparing to face Apollo Creed, children started running with him, all of them jumping up and down, arms stretched overhead atop the Art Museum steps.

The Wildcats weren't exactly Rocky. But they were close, a team delivering a hero moment in the most dramatic fashion.

"I've never seen anything like it," said Arcidiacono, who attended the Phillies parade years earlier as a fan.

Philadelphia mayor Jim Kenney, a La Salle graduate, introduced Wright and his team and said he picked his alma mater's Big 5 rival to win the championship.

"Personally, for the first time in my life, I picked Villanova to go all the way," he said. "And I won my bracket, so thank you. And one other thing: if you want to come back next year, come on back. We'll be waiting for you."

The players each took turns speaking, juniors Jenkins and Hart greeted with chants of "One more year," fans imploring them to finish their Villanova careers instead of heading straight for the NBA.

Finally Wright took the microphone. He led chants and cheers as always, but then summed up the enormity of the afternoon, how the parade was driving home Villanova's reality, perfectly.

"When we were on the court and Kris hit the shot and the streamers came down, that was a dream come true, something you could never imagine," he said. "But when we came down on Market Street right here and saw all of these people, that shocked us more than that shot. We want to thank you for making our dream come true today. This is amazing."

The big screens assembled behind the team then replayed the final seconds, and as Jenkins' shot went in, Philadelphia hoops fans responded in the most perfect Philadelphia way. At Big 5 games, fans once threw streamers onto the court after the first made basket before the NCAA banned the tradition. Just as the video showed Jenkins' game winner, the people in Dillworth Plaza tossed streamers in the air.

"The whole day was just amazing," Ochefu said.

And yet the Wildcats party still wasn't over.

When Wright first started at Villanova, the university hosted the team's annual awards banquet at the Villanova Room of the Connelly Center. It held around 400 people, more than adequate space for the alumni, boosters, and former players who wished to attend. Two weeks after the parade, Villanova welcomed some 1,600 people to the Pavilion for a cocktail reception and banquet honoring its 2016 team.

Television screens behind the stage played the championship game in its entirety as people milled about, many seeking out the players and coaches for pictures. The formal part of the banquet was set to start but the video of the game hadn't quite reached the finish. Master of ceremonies Scott Graham wisely decided to allow the game to play out until its epic conclusion before beginning his remarks.

He then turned the microphone over to Father John Stack, the vice president for student life and a longtime basketball fan, for the benediction.

"Let's bow our heads for 4.7 seconds," Stack began.

So went the theme of the evening, a reliving of that glorious game as well as a good-bye to some of the people who made it happen. Former players were introduced and awards given out, but the highlight of the night belonged to the seniors. Each spoke—Patrick Farrell, Kevin Rafferty, and Henry Lowe, the walk-ons, going first—before giving way to Ochefu and finally Arcidiacono.

The two masterminds of Villanova's triumphant turnaround, the ones who spearheaded the Redemption Class through the heartache of NCAA Tournament disappointment to a final play that could only be realized by their selflessness, were both overcome with emotion.

Ochefu thanked everyone he could think of, from the Villanova professors who "treated me like a real person," to the facilities people who "gave me an extra scoop of food." He singled out JayVaughn Pinkston, a graduate from the year before who Ochefu had leaned on heavily for leadership and guidance, and then turned to his team-mates. Pausing to gather himself, he spoke directly to them, recalling how a year before he'd toyed with leaving college early for the NBA. He questioned his decision to stay through the summer and fall, even into the beginning part of his senior season.

"Did I make the right decision? Was it worth it?" he said. "Well to be here, at this point, I can say it was worth it."

Ochefu then chided Hart, a junior who still hadn't officially decided to return to school. "Josh, I'm sorry to put this pressure on you, but I'm Team One More Year as well. It's worth it," he said.

Finally the senior turned his attention to Wright. Wiping away tears as he spoke, he recalled his mother's charge to Wright when Ochefu's career began—that she was handing over a rough stone and she expected him to return a diamond.

"As a basketball player, I'm still a rough stone," Ochefu said. "But as a man, I am that diamond of a man my mom wanted me to be."

He finished speaking, worried that he would break down entirely, before letting Arcidiacono have the last word. The player who had come to define the program and personify the way Wright wanted his players to compete thanked a host of people, just as Ochefu did. He singled out his older sister, Sabrina, the one who cried when she thought he would go to Florida instead of Villanova. He thanked his mother, Patti, for letting him shoot on his Fisher-Price net in the living room, even if meant a few broken picture frames. He fought back tears, trying to explain the sacrifices and support his father, Joe, had given him. He apologized to his siblings for not being around to do his share of chores and to athletic trainer Jeff Pierce for giving him too much work.

"I don't know how many stitches I had and you constantly told me to stop but it's not what we do at Villanova, it's not what I do," Arcidiacono said of Pierce. "We jump over every table, so I'm sorry."

Struggling to keep his composure, Arcidiacono's voice cracked as he remembered Bobby Taggart, a 17-year-old boy with cancer who connected to the Wildcats via Team IMPACT, a charitable organization. Taggart initially joined the team on January 22, 2013, as the Wildcats were mired in a three-game losing skid and about to face fifth-ranked Louisville. Villanova won that game and Taggart, quickly dubbed the team's good-luck charm, became a part of the Villanova family. A regular at games and practices, Taggart lost his fight with cancer on November 8, 2015, just days before the Wildcats' championship season was set to begin.

"He was a big help in our run to this national championship," a teary-eyed Arcidiacono said, pausing twice to collect himself.

Finally, Arcidiacono, like Ochefu, turned to address his head coach last. The point guard had been dubbed a mini Jay Wright, and he joked that he "always wanted to be Ryan Wright."

"You took a chance on a kid that sat out his senior year and always told me I would have a scholarship even if I couldn't play," Arcidiacono said, recalling his time mending from serious back surgery. "That gave me the free mindset to just play and not worry, and I can't thank you enough."

Then Arcidiacono wiped the tears out of his eyes and smiled as he thanked the university for the best four years of his life. "Once a Wildcat, always a Wildcat. Go Cats!" he said.

It was the perfect coda to end the celebration of an epic year.

Except the never-ending party still wasn't over.

On May 31, the Wildcats boarded yet another bus and headed south on Interstate 95. This time they stopped at 1600 Pennsylvania Avenue, also known as the White House, to pay a visit to President Barack Obama.

Wide-eyed and clearly overwhelmed, the Wildcats enjoyed a private tour of parts of the White House before meeting individually with the president.

"What's up Big Shot?" Obama said to Jenkins behind closed doors.

Finally the team was ushered into a packed East Room for the public reception with the president.

The largest room in the executive mansion, the East Room is frequently used for public gatherings and private parties. Theodore Roosevelt's daughter, Alice, was married there and President Abraham Lincoln used the space to host a party for Ulysses S. Grant before Grant was named chief of the Union Army. Decorated in heavy gold curtains and ornate chandeliers, the room's history practically seeps through the walls.

The Wildcats were arranged on risers behind a podium and waited patiently for Obama to arrive. A basketball fan himself, Obama admitted he had chosen wrong, picking Kansas to win the national championship. Vice President Joe Biden, who had attended the Final Four, picked the Wildcats.

"Unfortunately, I didn't go with his counsel and my bracket was busted," Obama said.

After introducing Wright as the "George Clooney" of college basketball coaches, the president lauded the team for more than the final shot, pointing out the team's willingness to dive for loose balls and play suffocating defense. He then introduced some of the players, pausing to ask Hart where he went to high school.

"Sidwell Friends," Hart replied.

Obama's daughter, Malia, would graduate from the same school in a matter of weeks.

He used Ochefu's nickname—the Chef—and Jenkins' Big Smoove moniker, too, before struggling to spit out Arcidiacono's name, mispronouncing the guard's name badly.

"Man, that's a lot of vowels in there, so I'm just going to call him Arch," Obama said.

The president went on to praise the team for its ability to survive North Carolina's furious comeback, relived the final play, and jokingly referred to Wright's too-cool reaction.

"That's what we saw from the Wildcats all season—a heart of a champion," he concluded.

Villanova presented Obama with a framed picture of him taking a shot that mirrored Jenkins' game winner as well as replica jerseys from a game they played in December, at Pearl Harbor.

The entire reception lasted no more than 15 minutes yet it clearly affected the players and coaches in attendance. At a brief press conference outside afterward, Arcidiacono forgave the president for butchering his name—"It's not every day the president of the United States mispronounces your name," he said—while Ochefu admitted he decided against trying to sneak a selfie with the president.

"I was too worried about the Secret Service agents," Ochefu said.

Hart said he could have met the president once before, when he visited Sidwell Friends, but Hart fell asleep in the school locker room. This time, he said, he came prepared, not just for the visit but sporting a red-white-and-blue bowtie for the occasion.

"I had it in my arsenal, just in case I needed it," Hart said.

And Wright, usually the picture of calm, was clearly overwhelmed by the trip. Moved that the president knew so much about his team, the coach struggled to explain what the experience meant.

"We've got a lot of respect for him as a great leader and a great man, but he's also a baller," Wright said. "He can play. He's cool."

So, too, it turned out, were the Cats.

At the time that the Wildcats were visiting the White House, a viral dance craze had taken over the country, especially popular among athletes. Started by two high school kids, the "Running Man Challenge" took off after two Maryland basketball players posted a video of themselves doing the dance moves to the 1996 Ghost Town DJ's song, "My Boo." Soon basketball players everywhere were trying to one up each other, posting their own Running Man Challenge videos from random sites around campus or on their practice courts.

At the urging of Ochefu and Jenkins, the Wildcats decided to do their own Running Man Challenge before they left the grounds. With the White House clearly in sight behind them and the players dressed in their presidential meet-and-greet finery, the entire team gathered for the video. Jenkins immediately posted it to his Instagram account with the tagline, "Officially ending this Runningman challenge. Presidential edition."

"We thought it would be cool to do it as a team," Jenkins said, adding that he was pretty sure no one would be able to top their effort.

It was, in fact, the perfect drop-the-mic finish to the Cats' season and, as it turned out, their last official act as a team.

The celebrating wouldn't end after the White House visit, but with graduation over and classes finished, the team would scatter afterward.

Jenkins headed home to Maryland, where he filled his bedroom with banners and posters and a huge flag declaring Villanova the national champions. It was, Jenkins admitted, slightly awkward, what with his brother, Nate Britt Jr., right next door. Britt, after all, only had Final Four gear from his North Carolina experience to decorate his space.

"He's been in my room twice since I got home," Jenkins laughed. "I think he tries to limit his visits."

In truth the relationship with his brother couldn't be better. The two talked immediately after the championship game, and as devastated as Britt was to not win, he couldn't have been happier to see Jenkins enjoy his moment. Britt even took Jenkins to the North Carolina campus in the early summer and let him in a pickup game. Later, Jenkins bumped into UNC coach Roy Williams.

"He was great," Jenkins said. "Told me it was a great shot."

Ochefu and Arcidiacono, meantime, first walked at graduation and then took off to chase their NBA dreams, Arcidiacono relocating to Maryland and Ochefu working out in California. Both were treated like movie stars in their final days of campus, stopped frequently while walking at graduation for pictures or autographs.

"I don't think I saw a sad face on campus for the rest of my senior year," Arcidiacono said.

Arcidiacono even signed an endorsement deal with a local car dealer and filmed a few commercials for the company.

His father, Joe—who was quick to remind his son his first car out of college was a Chevy Nova with 100,000 miles and no air conditioning—drove him to pick up his new car, a 2016 Range Rover. Along the way Arcidiacono asked his dad if he'd get the same deal his older siblings received; after graduating college, Joe had paid their car insurance for two years, helping them to ease into the transition of paying their bills.

"I said, 'Ry, that was like 40 bucks a month, not 200 or whatever this is going to be,'" Joe said. "And he goes, 'Well that's not right.' Meantime I'm driving an old minivan and he's trying to get drafted."

Arcidiacono wasn't drafted but later signed a free-agent deal with the San Antonio Spurs. The two-year deal is partially guaranteed.

Ochefu signed a similar, three-year partially guaranteed contract with the Washington Wizards. On the few occasions he was home, Ochefu enjoyed a house decorated much like Jenkins' bedroom—championship gear everywhere. During his NBA workouts and later at the summer-league games in Las Vegas, he was stunned by how many coaches and players knew who he was—more than a few called him Champ.

"They all wanted to dissect the play," Ochefu said. "They wanted to know how we did it."

Back home, Ochefu didn't quite enjoy the same treatment. Instead, whenever his mother spied a dirty floor, Elizabeth Ochefu would harken back to her son's championship actions and quip, "Oh leave it. Daniel can mop it."

No one received the star treatment quite like Wright, though. It seemed the coach was out of his office more than he was in, meeting with alumni groups and various companies, escorting some of his players to ring the bell at the New York Stock Exchange, others to receive the Wanamaker Award from the city of Philadelphia, and another group to Los Angeles for the ESPYs. Nominated for four of the sports awards, the Wildcats didn't win any—plenty of people took to social media, lamenting that Aaron Rodgers' Hail Mary pass in Green Bay's win against Detroit won the best play award over Jenkins' final shot—but they enjoyed the literal red-carpet treatment at the show.

Even as late as August, a good four months after the championship, Wright's Twitter feed showed the coach posing for pictures with various marketing companies and car dealers, finishing up a photo shoot for *GQ* magazine, and taking part in a video with the Philadelphia Flyers.

That, of course, doesn't include his day job of prepping the Wildcats for the next season. Along with the regular busy July recruiting schedule, Wright helped coach the USA Select Team in Las Vegas as it prepped to head to Rio de Janeiro for the Olympics.

"My concern always is Coach's time," Dunleavy said. "Can we take something off your plate? Can we attend an event so you can go out to dinner with the players or spend time with your family?"

But wise from his last run, Wright was very aware of the demands on his time and recognized the difference between doing things that he had to do and doing things he wanted to do. And having been through all of the NCAA Tournament disappointments following the 2009 Final Four run, he also knew how fleeting such attention could be.

"We're going to enjoy the hell out of this," he said.

And he did, as did seemingly everyone else even peripherally attached to Villanova. In suburbs and beach towns, in downtown Center City brownstones and on the Main Line estates, more and more homes were flying their Villanova flags. Where once Philadelphia and its surrounding area were filled with people proudly wearing their Penn State gear, now everyone had a Villanova T-shirt. It was as if the entire area discovered its inner Villanova fandom.

The euphoria stretched across the summer, carrying in to early August when Villanova hosted its annual Summer Jam. The carnival is usually considered an early kickoff to the next season, a chance for fans to meet their future Wildcats and get a sneak peak of what lies ahead.

At the 2016 Summer Jam, fans were even treated to an intrasquad scrimmage. Villanova was traveling to Spain the next day for a week-long tour where they'd play professional teams. By NCAA rules, they were allowed to practice and scrimmage together in the days ahead. This, then, was the first glimpse at big-time freshman Omari Spellman, the first time to watch Hart and Jenkins assume their roles as leaders, to see Jalen Brunson run the show without benefit of Arcidiacono's leadership.

But rather than serve as a jumpstart for Villanova's future, Summer Jam was just an extension of the celebration of the recent past. Darryl Reynolds, Phil Booth, Brunson, Hart, and Jenkins—the returning players from the championship team—were greeted with the loudest rounds of applause.

Wright tried to move things along. He greeted fans enthusiastically but cautioned them that while they were free to enjoy the championship, his team was moving forward. He didn't want to talk about the 2016 season any longer, didn't want to even relive the final shot.

His players echoed the same refrain. They insisted that, as amazing and wonderful as the national championship experience had been, it was time to put the whole thing in the rearview mirror. They had stopped watching replays of the game, no longer rewound the final 4.7 seconds again and again to marvel at the epic finish.

They were putting 2016, they said, to bed.

"We're not national champions anymore," Hart said. "We understand that. We're not listening to any of that stuff in the outside world. That's behind us. Other people want to talk about the championship game. We don't talk about it. It's over."

After a summer of social media shout outs from rap stars and NBA All-Stars, from national television appearances to more selfie requests than he could count, even Jenkins, the architect of the last-second drama, stood inside the media room at Villanova's Pavilion on a hot August evening and said he had officially put his heroics behind him.

"That shot will stay with me for the rest of my life. It's something I'll never forget," he said. "But I've got to move forward."

Epilogue

Tucked into a small booth at a Dunkin Donuts near his Langhorne, Pennsylvania, home, Joe Arcidiacono had just finished reliving Villanova's journey over the last four years when he had to stop himself, as if what he had said had finally resonated.

Collecting himself finally, Arcidiacono grinned.

"It should be a movie," he said. "But no one would believe the finish."

Indeed, it is *Hoosiers* mixed with *Rudy* topped off, fittingly, with just a hint of *Rocky*.

The end, of course, is what makes a movie and Villanova staged its final scene perfectly, with Kris Jenkins swishing a game-winning three-pointer just as the buzzer sounded. So good was the ending that after he removed his headset, Bill Raftery immediately sought out the opinion of one man. For nearly 30 years, Bob Fishman has served as the lead director for the CBS broadcast of the NCAA Tournament. He worked his first championship game in 1982, when a kid by the name of Michael Jordan hit a game winner as North Carolina beat Georgetown. Fishman is the go-to guy for Raftery, and plenty of others, when it comes to putting games in historical context.

"This was the best game I've ever been a part of," Raftery remembered Fishman saying. "That," Raftery added, "is pretty impressive."

But it is the arc of the entire Villanova season, completed by that remarkable ending, that makes this championship run so unforgettable. While Jay Wright and his incoming 2016–17 roster insisted at their August Summer Jam that they had closed the book on the national championship season, plenty of others would reread the final chapter until they committed it to memory. It was, like all great novels, too good to put down. Except, of course, it wasn't fiction. Impossibly, improbably, it had all happened.

A long shot is defined as a "venture or guess that has only the slightest chance of succeeding or being accurate." On the surface Villanova, with its 29 regular-season wins, onetime No. 1 ranking, and second seed in the NCAA Tournament, didn't fit the definition. If anything, the Wildcats looked an awful lot like favorites.

But even in sports, a world governed by statistics and analytics, numbers don't necessarily tell the whole story. This was a Villanova team known more for losing big games than winning them. This was a program competing from the wrong side of the financial ledger in a college sports era where money talked. This was a team competing for a league that boldly decided a basketball-centric conference could compete in a football-dominated world. And this was a roster without a single silver-spoon-tasting, Easy Street–riding member, including the head coach.

Jay Wright had had to reinvent himself midway through his career, falling so hard from the pinnacle of a 2009 Final Four appearance that outsiders questioned his coaching acumen. Ryan Arcidiacono, who would come to be the face of the program, was once a suburban kid with a bad back considered a step too slow for the big time, who only opted for Villanova because his big sister bawled when he suggested he might go elsewhere. Daniel Ochefu, the other team captain, was an undersized big man whose value to the team was never properly regarded because of the talented guards surrounding him, a player who only came to basketball after taking a soccer detour across the world. And Kris Jenkins, raised by strangers who became his family, arrived in college overweight, out of shape, lightly recruited, and a little too nervy even for his shoot-'em-up-or-sleep-in-the-streets-preaching head coach.

No, this team was not supposed to win a national championship.

"We never felt like underdogs," Arcidiacono said. "But I guess other people thought we were."

Because the Wildcats were. Before Villanova, the last team to win a championship from outside college basketball's perceived elite programs was...Villanova. And that had been 31 years ago. In the years between the Wildcats' Cinderella 1985 championship and their long shot 2016 title, 16 schools had traded the NCAA championship back and forth, UNLV and Arkansas ranking as the closest thing to outliers. Duke, Connecticut, Kansas, Kentucky, and North Carolina alone combined for 17 of those 30 trophies.

In that span, the game had changed and changed drastically, football directly influencing college basketball and the freshest (as in freshmen) talent winning more frequently.

Villanova, with no big-time football and just one McDonald's All-American, was a square peg trying to swish a shot through the round-holed basket.

In 2016 the Wildcats essentially reshaped the college basketball landscape. Long dogged by critics because they couldn't escape the NCAA Tournament's first weekend, the Wildcats answered them by demolishing their early NCAA opponents. Once told they couldn't compete with the top dogs of their sport they, in order, dispatched of heavy tournament favorite Kansas, player of the year Buddy Hield, and college basketball demigod North Carolina. Along the way Villanova took a fledgling Big East Conference on its back and carried it to the top and proved that a coach known for his haberdashery ought to be respected for his smarts.

Above all else, in a world gone reality star mad with the exploits of individuals, the 2016 Villanova Wildcats showed the priceless value of team in one selfless, unforgettable play.

A screen, a pass, a shot, and a championship.

Villanova 77, North Carolina 74.

"That," Ochefu said, "was the ultimate Villanova play."

A play called Nova that defined a team and redefined a program.

Acknowledgments

I was standing on the court at NRG Stadium, trying not to trip over the confetti strewn all over the floor, when a friend grabbed my arm.

"You've got to write a book," he said.

At the moment I was too worried about writing a game story that would do justice to the drama I had just witnessed to even contemplate a book. But when the confetti and my head both cleared, I thought a little harder about it. Before joining ESPN.com, I spent eight years at the *Philadelphia Daily News*, six as the Villanova basketball beat writer. I was there the day Jay Wright was introduced as the head coach, and I was in the cafeteria when he stood on the tables to drum up interest in his team. I covered the phone code fiasco and the NCAA investigation, and at our annual preseason breakfast, I once asked Wright what it felt like to be on the hot seat.

The more I thought about it, the more I realized that if I were to walk into a bookstore and see someone else had written a book about this national championship run, I'd be disappointed.

Maybe, as my friend suggested, I ought to write a book.

From thought to execution, though, there are a lot of steps and even more people who helped. So I guess the best place to start with my endless list of thanks is with my friend who sent me down this crazy path: Pat Forde of Yahoo!Sports. He's the one who grabbed me after the title game and planted the idea in my head. He then listened to me whine when the idea gave way to the cold, hard reality of writing. I am lucky to have a lot of friends in journalism, but even luckier to be inspired by so many amazing colleagues. Pat is one of them. Another is my dear friend Dick Jerardi of the *Philadelphia Daily News*. I have long said I learned half of what I know about journalism and basketball (and horse racing) riding in the car alongside Jerardi. I am indebted to him, to Pat, and others such as Shannon Ryan of the *Chicago Tribune* and Rick Bozich of WDRB in Louisville, for their friendship, support, and daily reminder of how to do this job well.

Of course, I also am fortunate to work with people cut of the same talented cloth, the folks at ESPN.com. My editor, Nick Pietruszkiewicz, seconded the idea that I write this book, his suggestion actually pushing the lark into a reality as he suggested I reach out to Jayson Stark, our esteemed baseball writer, for some guidance. Thanks to Jayson for telling me I could actually do this and to Nick, as well as Chad Millman and Mary Byrne at ESPN.com, for green-lighting the opportunity.

Unless otherwise noted, all of the interviews here were conducted by me, either for the book specifically or in my other life as a reporter for ESPN.com and the *Daily News*. Of course, information-gathering these days includes a lot of Google, so I'd be remiss if I didn't mention the sources I culled some background from: ESPN.com, the *Philadelphia Daily News*, the *Philadelphia Inquirer*, the *Delaware County Times*, *The New York Times*, the Big East Conference, Villanova University, basketball-reference.com, ASAPSports.com, CBSSports.com, csnphilly.com, yahoosports.com, USATodaysports.com, and *Sports Illustrated*.

To the people who graciously took the time to answer my questions: Baker Dunleavy, Kris Jenkins, Ryan Arcidiacono, Daniel Ochefu, Mikal Bridges, Mouphtaou Yarou, Kyle Lowry, Father Rob Hagan, John

Shackleton, Joe Arcidiacono, Nate Britt Sr., Felicia Jenkins, Elizabeth Ochefu, Vince Nicastro, Ed Pinckney, Bill Raftery, Val Ackerman, Mike Tranghese, Mike Mikulski, Derek Wright, Billy Lange, Patrick Chambers, Joe Jones, Pat Flannery, Speedy Claxton, Seth Berger, Billy Donovan, Andy Katz, Pat Forde, and Dick Jerardi—I thank you and hope I did your stories justice.

To my niece, Kelly Pennett, the world's greatest transcriber, thank you for your patience while listening to endless hours of interviews and also for saying you even enjoyed them.

I also am indebted to Michael Sheridan, the sports information director at Villanova University, who not only helped set up interviews with Villanova players and staff, but graciously answered emails and phone calls along the way.

And of course thanks to Jay Wright for graciously opening the doors to his program. His lone charge to me was, "I don't want this to be about me," which, of course isn't exactly easy to do. I tried.

I wrote this book at Long Beach Island, New Jersey, where my family is lucky enough to spend the summer. Writing a book at the beach is not necessarily the greatest way to enjoy, or even regularly see, the ocean, so a special shout out to my LBI posse who helped me keep my sanity: Karen and Bill Eng, Meg and Matt Bingham, and Kris Cauda. Additional thanks for the constant reality checks to my at-home crew, Pete and MaryLou Sienko, and Matt and Lynne Coulter.

From my mother, Graceann, a former English teacher, I learned to love the written word. From my father, Donald, a onetime college baseball player and longtime Yankees fan (and occasional sufferer), I learned to love sports. I thank both of them for giving me my career.

Finally to my husband, George, and my children, Madigan and Kieran, thanks for putting up with me, for encouraging me and quite literally cheering me through the home stretch. I love you all.

About the Author

Dana O'Neil is a senior writer for ESPN.com, where she primarily covers men's college basketball. A past president of the United States Basketball Writers Association, she worked previously at the *Philadelphia Daily News, Bucks County Courier Times, Florida Times-Union*, and *The Trentonian*. Dana is a Penn State University graduate and lives in Newtown, Pennsylvania, with her husband, George, her children, Madigan and Kieran, and her dog, Maisy.